A CHRISTIAN'S ROADMAP

BIBLICAL LESSONS WE'VE LEARNED
BUT FORGOTTEN

BY: BOB MCCULLOUGH, LCSW

Copyright © 2013 by Bob McCullough, LCSW

A Christian's Roadmap
Biblical Lessons We've Learned But Forgotten

by Bob McCullough, LCSW

Printed in the United States of America

ISBN 9781628713510

All rights reserved solely by the author. The author guarantees all contents are original and do not infringe upon the legal rights of any other person or work. No part of this book may be reproduced in any form without the permission of the author. The views expressed in this book are not necessarily those of the publisher.

Unless otherwise indicated, Bible quotations are taken from the New International Version (NIV). Copyright © 1996 by Zondervan.

www.xulonpress.com

TABLE OF CONTENTS

Introduction..v
Story Telling 7
Giants 17
Sin 23
Doubt..32
Fighting Evil 37
Grace..41
Humility 49
Love 53
Parenting...61
Patiently Waiting..71
Politics..77
Suffering 87
Trust 93
Character and Image 100
Godly Men 107
Random Thoughts...115
Beginning 119
Recommended Readings 121

INTRODUCTION

There are thousands of self-help books to assist you on many different topics: lose weight, gain muscle, look younger, become rich, be a better parent, spouse, employee, manager, etc. We spend millions of dollars each year reading these books and attending seminars in order to live better or be happier. As a counselor, I have read many of these books and attended the seminars and always leave feeling inspired and motivated but yet never completely fulfilled or understand my purpose or *why* I should try to live better.

During my experience as a counselor, I have worked with many different populations: children, adults, families, marriage, premarital, divorce, blended families, crisis intervention and trauma. I have seen just about every type of incident that can happen to one of these groups but I felt like there was only so much I could do to help. I know the different theories, the book work, what the manual says to do but as a counselor I can only get you so far. I needed to realize that the greatest counselor is Jesus; the Bible is our manual for life and provides all we need to learn how to live.

Special thanks needs to go out to Pastor Tom Holladay at Saddleback Church. I began to listen to Pastor Holladay's Drivetime Devotions and had completed several of the series before I came upon the Book of Romans study. While I had read through the bible before, Pastor Tom's insight had me experiencing in ways I had not previously. I also need to give special thanks to Chuck Swindoll with whom I listen to every morning on my way into the office. There is just something about his style, humor and honesty that helps me understand what God is saying. There are many great bible teaching pastors out there and I will mention some of them as resources throughout this book.

While much of the inspiration for this book comes from Romans, we will look at other books in the bible as well as other resources. The goal is to take a look at many of the issues that we face every day and see how the bible tells us we should handle those situations. I also want to make sure that we look at resources so where appropriate these will be listed for you to explore further.

Finally, I am not a biblical scholar with many degrees in theology. I am a counselor with over 20 years' experience who happens to be a Christian and continues to learn every day the power of God's love and guidance through His word. I have hope that this book provides you with a different tool with which to draw closer to the plan that God has for you.

STORY TELLING

Genesis 1:1 In the beginning God created the heavens and the earth.

And thus begins God's story. We will talk about story telling further in the chapter on parenting but I wanted to devote time here to the telling of individual's personal walk of faith. One of the precepts we have in responding to disasters and assisting individuals recover from a critical incident is that everyone has a story to tell. It is important that this is story is told for many reasons: process events and emotions; begin the healing process; use your story to help others. If you are a Christian, you have a story to tell. Your story tells of how you came to know God, the decision points along the journey, the people that came along side you and what your daily walk looks like. Your ability to tell this story can be so impactful to new believers or non-believers because you make it real.

As we begin this book I want you to hear the stories of a few real people. Listen to the tone, the words and the impact that God has had on their life. Note, having a personal relationship with God, being filled with the Holy Spirit and knowing Jesus as your savior does not mean there will not be any trouble or dark days. What it means is that you have security in knowing eternity is prepared for you.

<u>Male – 17 years old</u>

I was raised in a Christian home, baptized at an early age and given opportunities to participate in many mission trips both domestic and international. My youth group is very important to me and I find many decisions regarding college focus on my ability to stay involved with this group that has helped mold me and allowed me to grow in my faith.

School has been a great opportunity to see God at work. I attend a large public high school and it is not always easy to know who is a Christian. However, I can feel the Holy Spirit at work guiding me and protecting me when temptation is near.

My parents have helped set the example for my walk with God. They have allowed me to grow by making mistakes but help me learn from the errors so I don't make them again.

As I prepare for college, I look forward to seeing the plans God has for me. I know there will be challenges and tough times but with God's direction I'm excited to see what happens next.

Female–62 years old

I have always loved the Lord. As a child, my Dad always took my older brother and sister and me to church every Sunday morning and night, and every Wednesday evening. We were raised Baptist, and I enjoyed being at the church. Seeing Jesus' picture in the posters on the walls or in the Sunday School books was a familiar and comforting feeling. When my brother and sister decided they were ready to be baptized, I thought I was ready, too, and joined them in "going forward". Steve was about 16, Carol was 15, and I was 10. Often I would take my cues from them, thinking they were smarter than me. After all, I did love Jesus and I knew he loved me. The song says it's so. As I got older and my brother and sister graduated and went off to college and work, I started questioning the need for "church" in my life. My Dad had always been my ride, but now he left the flock over a dispute with one of the deacons, and I really didn't have the commitment level I needed to seek out another way to get myself to church. I was a teenager and needed a strong influence to keep me in the boundaries of my Christian walk. It wasn't there. I met my husband when I was a senior and he had just graduated. He had been raised a Baptist in the same neighborhood as me, and had also wandered off the path, with no one reaching out to him. We figured we were "good" kids, and even attended different churches a couple of times, just to see if we would fit in. We never did connect anywhere, so we basically quite the search. We still attended church service on the holidays, usually with my older brother and his family.

We had our friends and a full life with both of us working and playing on the weekends. Our friends were "good" people, too, and we have many fond memories of experiences we all share. However, some of the activities we enjoyed then are not anything we would tolerate now. Our partying habits and lack of any involvement with a church, or even praying, were shameful at best. As someone who had been raised differently, I knew better. There was always a still small voice in my head that would tell me to stop all this and turn back to Jesus.

When I became pregnant with my first child, I knew I needed to treat my body better and be healthy for my baby. My husband, on the other hand, did not see the need to change any of his habits. An instinct in me was telling me that we needed to provide a better environment in our home for our new family. This is when that still small voice in my head became a little louder. Our marriage had always been rocky, and now it seemed to get even rougher. Hind sight shows me now that as I was being called to come back to Christ, this was making David more uncomfortable. He apparently was not having that same conversation.

Now, that voice in my head was getting really annoying, and I couldn't ignore it any longer. One day in my kitchen, when my two sweet children were outside playing, I sat at my kitchen table and had it out with that voice. That voice had all the answers, and between my crying and confessing and asking for forgiveness, that voice became the sweetest sound I ever heard. I stopped holding back from God, and surrendered everything I had to him, even my children. Earlier that winter, I had started talking to David about getting back into church, and he was absolutely not interested, and went as far as to say the children would not be going, either. Knowing that he felt that way, the voice asked me if I would still commit myself to serving Him. I felt guilty to say that I would leave my babies behind, but the voice was adamant when telling me that I needed to make myself right before I could be any good for them. I trusted Him and agreed to put us in His hands.

That next Sunday, I got up early to get ready for church, and planned to get the children ready as well. I had asked David the day before to come with me to church that day. He said nothing in reply. As I was getting all of us ready, I expected…something, an argument, doors being slammed, crying. Instead, David got up and got ready to come with us. He didn't say anything, so I just went about getting us all in the car, and we drove to church. It was the church my brother went to so he and his family were, excited to see us. As we sat through the service, I knew I would be "going forward" to join, and anticipated some animosity from David. When it was time to step out of our pew, David stood and followed me up to where the pastor was standing. We both joined that day. That's God's amazing grace!! I trusted Him, and he promised He would take care of everything. I once was lost, but now I am found. He never left me from the time I was a small girl loving His pictures on the walls in my Sunday School class. I had left Him. I thank my Father in Heaven for never giving up on me.

Fifty years later, I "went forward" and asked to be baptized again. This time, I know why I am doing it. It's because I understand now what loving God really means. What it really means to have God love me.

Female – 58 years old

I was born to very conservative Christian parents and attended church every Sunday from that time on! We were members of a First Christian Church, Disciples of Christ. When I was 11 years old, I accepted Christ as my Lord and Savior and was baptized on Easter Sunday. During this whole time, my mother was suffering from health issues and had some mental issues and was very, very cross with me. She loved me, but had no idea how to show that and I couldn't do much right for her. Even if I did, she would not have told me. By the time I was a teenager, I turned very rebellious. Although I knew there was a line I couldn't cross, I pushed life right up to the edge. Through a number of circumstances during the next few years, I was not only very angry with my mother, but I decided if it was this bad with God, I didn't need Him. I chose to walk my own road for a few years and I found out what life was like without God. On top of other things, I ended up married to a man who was not a Christian and not faithful. I can honestly say that it didn't matter what I did, I felt the Lord tugging at my heart and trying to coax me back to his side. I felt Him in my heart the whole time and eventually, I was so miserable and hurting, I cried out to him. I wrote down all of the sins I had committed during those years, tore them into pieces and put them in a bowl, praying through tears the whole time. I took a match and lit the papers and immediately the papers were engulfed in one big flame and suddenly ashes. I felt totally exhausted and lay down on my bed. I was still praying and giving him praise and I had a feeling of water running through my entire body. I believe it was the cleansing of the Holy Spirit. I fell asleep after that, but when I got up the next morning, I knew I was saved and filled with the Holy Spirit. He had forgiven me of all the bad stuff I had confessed and consumed the written papers to show me they were ashes now. I knew it was true that He will not let you go, even when you stray. He has kept me strong through a divorce after almost 20 years of marriage and being a single mom and through quite a few heart breaks and challenges. Giving my life back to Him did not mean life was easy, but since that night, I surrender everything to Him and keep on moving forward. The hardest thing I had to learn was that God loves me. When I discovered I needed to know that, it became a true search to make myself believe He does. He is very patient with me and even though it's been quite a long time, we are still taking things one step at a time! I know I am a child of the King and I am worth something! I love him and I am growing in His word and understanding, and I am walking through my life behind His leading and surrounded by his arms of love.

Female – 66 years old

I am a 66 year old woman who by the Grace of God has been saved from the eternal punishment due me and this is my story.

I was baptized at the age of 5 because my parents were pressured by my uncle who was a priest to baptize my brother and me. My parents never went to church but would drop us off in front of church and pick us up after it was over.

We were sent off and on to Catholic schools and then later I was married in the church. I became disillusioned with the church when it went through the reformation so I quit attending.

My greatest regret in life was not raising my children with any Christian teaching. If I had known then what I know now that would all be different. This was one of my greatest sins I have asked God to forgive.

Without God in my life, I found myself totally lost and miserable. My life was in shambles. I felt completely alone and totally hopeless. And in the end, I became suicidal. As I lay on my bed with the TV on pretending to watch it while all the while I was trying to find a way to kill myself and make it look like an accident so my children would never know, God reached down and touched me through a TV evangelist. He preached the Bible and encouraged everyone to read it. So for the first time in my life I read the Bible. And there I found Christ and my whole life changed.

Over the years I learned more and more about Christ by reading His Word everyday, praying constantly throughout the day, and trying to find ways to serve Him. You will be surprised at what doors He will open for you when you open yourself up to His calling.

One of His greatest blessings to me is that for a long time I prayed that God would send someone to me that I could bring to Him. I didn't know how to go about evangelizing so

I just prayed. And you won't believe this, but He sent someone straight to my door! One day this lady I had only met once in my condo complex knocked on my door and said "I know you are a Christian, will you pray for me?" I said "Come on in....."

Eventually she joined my women's Bible study and then went to church with me. I was amazed. I didn't ask again until about 10 years later–God would you please send me someone else and again a new neighbor came over to chat. She said "I can tell you are a Christian woman. I have never gone to church." Well you can guess what I said–"Would you like to go with me?" She did and I watched her accept Christ as her Lord and Savior. I am praying again–God will you send someone to me? Wonder what He will say...

One of the most awesome evidences of Him watching over me was when crime moved into my condo complex and took over. I felt God asking me to trust Him and get the crime out of there so He could move in again. So reluctantly I said OK God. I will do what you lead me to do but you have to protect me and He did. I never had called the police in my life until then. The 1st few times I was trembling when I made the calls but then the police and I became great friends and worked together. We got rid of 5 drug dealers, 2 gangs, 2 thieves, and a number of vandals. It took 2 years but God, my prayer warriors; I and the police did it. Then I was able to get my pastor to have an outreach program started in my area. None of that would have happened if I didn't trust God to protect me.

Over the years I prayed that God will bring my children to him whom I failed so miserably. I have seen 2 of my 3 sons come to Christ along with all 3 daughter-in-laws and my 7 grandchildren. I am still praying for that last child and will never stop praying until he too is saved. I have faith God will save him and I anxiously wait to see it. God has truly blessed me even though I do not deserve it.

I know He is with me every day and with the ones I love. I know He has forgiven me for my sins, and they are many, but He loves me and I love Him. I pray daily that He will walk with each of my children and grandchildren so that they will have His love, peace and joy to get through life.

I will never leave Him again. He is my life.

<u>Steve and Heather</u>

2 Corinthians 6:14 (ESV) says "Do not be unequally yoked with unbelievers. For what partnership has righteousness with lawlessness? Or what fellowship has light with

darkness?" Along with that 1 Corinthians 15:33 (ESV) "Do not be deceived: "Bad company ruins good morals." These bring the reasoning for the second most important relationship in your life on earth; the spouse you choose.

I came to know Christ as many at a very young age. I walked the walk and made all the proper motions that made those around me think I was a "Christian." It was not until I was almost forty that I truly came to know Jesus Christ. How did my life with Christ change? I became "Equally Yoked" here on earth. I married the love of my life, Heather.

We were both married previously to nonbelievers. We found one another on the Internet before the Internet was. I am a nerd and she is just ever so much more. We found each other via emails, before Google, Facebook, even before "social media" was in our collective vocabulary. I will make this short; we found one another only through God's providence. He miraculously put us together to become one.

Heather was given a Bible when she was young; however, it was not until we began our lives together in prayer, study and attending worship together that she began to understand Christ's love and forgiveness. So together, we listened, we heard, we began to understand, we truly believed and understood who Christ is and what He did and why. With study and long deep discussions with my "equally yoked" spouse, along with the Holy Spirit, Christ became real.

It was around this time that I really began to know who Christ was. I could feel and hear the Holy Spirit moving and guiding myself and Heather's life towards His goals. Life became less about me and my selfish needs and more about Him. You know what the best part of all this was? It is easy.

There are so many "self-help" books on this or that telling you how to improve. Christ is easy. His Yoke is light as He carries it. We as humans try and make it all about the rituals and the procedures. God wants nothing but the adoration He deserves. That's it. Share Christ with your equally yoked partner and dreams become reality.

My story

I was not brought up in a Christian dedicated home. I say dedicated because both my parents would describe themselves as Christian but definitely not practicing their faith. I would attend vacation bible school sometimes and we would sometimes go to a Christmas service but we were far from actively engaged. My attitude during the child and teenage years was that I wanted to do good to stay out of trouble, make good grades and play sports. My relationship with God was definitely not a priority.

One of the things I find is that there are many decision points along the walk with God. One of the early decision points for me was during my mid teenage years. My mom became very involved in a church that had a great impact of our family. It caused much dissension and division between her and my dad and essentially the outcome for my brother's and I was to move farther away from God. I saw her faith as a barrier to our family and was certainly not positive.

Fortunately, the next major decision point in my walk occurred when I married a wonderful Christian woman and we started our family. For the first two years of our marriage we did not attend church regularly. Even though she was raised in a home that knew Jesus, it was not a top priority for us. After working all week sleeping in on Sunday morning sounded like a much better option. But then we had our first child and moved into a home we built. It was a new area for us with new neighbors that were all in similar stages of their life: newly married, starting to have children, and trying to figure out life. My wonderful wife informed me that we would be raising our children up in the church because she felt it was important that they have that relationship and it was something she needed to get back. Being a wise husband and counselor, I of course gave in thinking that it would not last. Figured she really did like her sleep and getting children ready to go 5 days a week was hard enough much less to do so on Sunday mornings. Fortunately for me, I was wrong and the schedule stuck.

We attended a few different churches looking for the one that we felt would be good for our family. Wanted to make sure the teaching was biblical and had to have a great children's program because that was most important to us at the time. As we continued to search, neighbor's let us know that they had found a church they really liked and had a great children's program. We decided to attend and found the children's program to be outstanding and the Senior Pastor, David McAlpin, to be a strong teacher of the bible. His teaching and style was unlike any other pastor I had listened and instead of thinking what I was going to have for lunch or which football game was on that day, I found myself paying attention and wanting to learn more.

The next decision point came during one of Dr. McAlpin's sermons where he was talking about counselors. Being my paid profession, I took notice because I wanted to see where he was going. He confirmed exactly what I had been feeling in my work: that worldly counseling can only take you so far but you need God to take you the rest of the way. It was true, I felt as if I could only help people make so much progress but complete healing, forgiveness and overcoming grief was going to come from a relationship with God. I had a conversation with Dr. McAlpin immediately following that sermon and thus began my first intense step with God.

Since then, I have truly felt God working in my life. I view decisions in a much different way, trying to focus on God's word and the plan he has for me. I also have felt the intense pressure of Satan and temptation. Before I was committed to God I don't think Satan cared but since then it feels like I am constantly tempted. Perhaps I'm more aware or perhaps it is intense focus that Satan places on God's children but it is there. I do know this: It is much easier for me to overcome temptation when I am in union with God. When I think I'm strong enough to resist temptation on my own, I lose every time.

On a daily basis I need to be fed. On days when the schedule is crazy with work, travel and kids sports schedules then it may be choosing to listen to a biblical program in the car or listen to worship music. But, that only satisfies in the short term. The opportunities to teach a class or be involved in a mission opportunity are where huge growth occurs for me. Staying committed to prayer, an open prayer that starts in the morning and goes all day is what I need to stay connected. It greatly helps me when I face temptation to have the Holy Spirit immediately guide me in the right direction (just wish I would always listen)!

I sometimes think back to what my life was like before this walk started. I was just going through the motions and had no sense of purpose or direction. That has all changed and I can't imagine my life without this journey. It truly gives comfort and reassurance to realize that God has a plan for me and the world. That with everything that is happening in this age, to know how it ends with evil defeated, gives me hope every day. My regret is that it took me so long to overcome myself and surrender to God so I can be free.

<u>Steve and Ruth</u>

Finally, I want to introduce to Steve and Ruth. They are extremely important to this book because at the end of each chapter you are going to read a personal application piece and for all but one of the chapters, Steve and Ruth have provided their thoughts. They are a great, God loving couple who have given so much of themselves and we have the privilege and honor to learn more throughout the book. I am very grateful for their friendship but more importantly their character. I hope and pray that everyone has a Steve and Ruth in their life that they can spend time learning and watching. Now, a bit about Steve and Ruth:

Steve is 68 years old and an engineer. Ruth is 66 years old, a RN and still volunteers her time at a free health clinic. They have been married 44 years with 3 children (ages 42, 38 and 33) and 4 grandchildren (ages 10, 8, 5 and 2). They have been involved in just about every church leadership position and continue to serve in the Stephens Ministry, Carpenter's for Christ and as a Deacon as well as other leadership roles.

GIANTS

1 Samuel 17:11 When Saul and his troops heard the Philistine's challenge, they were terrified and lost all hope.

We're not talking about the New York or San Francisco Giants for all you sports fans out there. We're talking about the giants that you face every day. Got to give credit to Bob Ingle and Max Lucado for some of the information in this message.

I'm sure that many if not all of you are familiar with the story of David and Goliath. Goliath was the 9 foot tall Philistine who for 40 days hurled insults at Israel challenging anyone of them to come and battle him. David is a teenage shepherd who has brought food to his brothers who are in Israel's army. He is not a warrior but he does have the confidence that God can overcome anything. The stakes: if Goliath wins, Israel becomes the slaves of the Philistines and if the Israelite won the Philistines would become Israel's slave.

The Philistine's are Israel's giant and Goliath is David's giant. Goliath is threatening David's way of life, his family, his country. For 40 days, Goliath has terrorized Israel, controlled them and scared the army so that no one would agree to fight against him. David arrives to deliver food to his brothers in the army and hears the insults that Goliath is hurling. Within just a few minutes, David tells King Saul:

1 Sam 17:32 "Let no one lose heart on account of this Philistine; your servant will go and fight him."

David has the confidence that God will protect him because he has in the past:

> *1 Samuel 17:36-37 David said, "I've been a shepherd, tending sheep for my father. Whenever a lion or bear came and took a lamb from the flock, I'd go after it, knock it down, and rescue the lamb. If it turned on me, I'd grab it by the throat, wring its neck, and kill it. Lion or bear, it made no difference—I killed it. And I'll do the same to this Philistine pig who is taunting the troops of God-Alive. GOD, who delivered me from the teeth of the lion and the claws of the bear, will deliver me from this Philistine."*

You know the rest of the story: David takes his slingshot and with one shot knocks Goliath to the ground where he then takes Goliath's own sword and cuts off his head. The rest of the Philistines are defeated and David becomes a national hero on his way to becoming King of Israel.

Now, this is a great story but how does it apply to us, today? Think about the giant that is facing you. Could be your health: chronic pain, cancer diagnosis, stress, depression, anxiety, getting older and the mind wants to but the body says no. Could be financial: lost job, retirement fund has taken a beating, bill collectors calling, kids need clothes and you don't know where the next meal is coming. Could be an addiction: gambling, drugs, alcohol, pornography. Could be anything: loveless marriage, poor relationship with your children, inappropriate relationship, caring for older parents while still taking care of young children. Could be a sin that you just cannot get past because you are so consumed that you will not let God in to show that you are forgiven.

This giant can be overwhelming; can consume everything that you do. It never leaves you, never lets you rest, keeps you from focusing on what is truly important. You feel tired, weak, perhaps guilt or remorse. You know what you should do but you do not have the strength or will power to do this on your own. You may feel like Israel and have no hope. Not only does the giant impact you personally, often times it impacts your family, friends and all other areas of your life.

Often times when we face a giant we feel as if nothing is going our way. The dark cloud continues to hang over us and we may think "what else could go wrong" and then it does. We keep battling, believing our luck is going to change but then the next thing happens and the next. Once we hit rock bottom is when we finally begin to look up. We have a tendency to surrender at this point and realize that what is happening is out of our control and we need to turn it over to God. We could have done this much earlier but as human's we love to try and control our destiny and circumstances. God has a way of throwing giants in front of us to bring us back to Him.

Look at where David is when he hits rock bottom with another giant he is facing, Saul:

Psalm 57 1:11 Have mercy on me, O God, have mercy on me, for in you my soul takes refuge. I will take refuge in the shadow of your wings until the disaster has passed. I cry out to God Most High, to God, who fulfills his purpose for me. He sends from heaven and saves me, rebuking those who hotly pursue me; God sends his love and his faithfulness. I am in the midst of lions; I lie among ravenous beasts—men whose teeth are spears and arrows, whose tongues are sharp swords. Be exalted, O God, above the heavens; let your glory be over all the earth. They spread a net for my feet—I was bowed down in distress. They dug a pit in my path—but they have fallen into it themselves. My heart is steadfast, O God, my heart is steadfast; I will sing and make music. Awake, my soul! Awake, harp and lyre! I will awaken the dawn. I will praise you, O Lord, among the nations; I will sing of you among the peoples. For great is your love, reaching to the heavens; your faithfulness reaches to the skies. Be exalted, O God, above the heavens; let your glory be over all the earth.

David realizes that he cannot overcome this on his own. He seeks God from the dark of the caves and cries out for God to fulfill David's purpose. David begins to have hope; he begins to sing and play music again because he has had an awakening in his soul. Note, Saul is still chasing him and trying to kill him but David has a new outlook on this new giant he is facing.

There are a few lessons that we can learn from David and Goliath that help us in facing our giant.

- Identify your giant. Don't dance around what controls you. Be honest with yourself and others and call the giant what it is. Denial can be a coping technique early on

when disaster strikes but you cannot stay there long term. Remember, you cannot begin to fight your giant until you know who or what you are battling.
- Ignore the negativity. David's brothers and Saul did not believe that he could fight and win against Goliath. Who is telling you that you cannot succeed? Who is telling you, "that's life, deal with it, move on." The last thing you need when facing a giant is to be surrounded by others telling you that the giant will win.
- Do not procrastinate. David did not waste any time. Goliath had been tormenting Israel for 40 days. Within a matter of moments, David is gathering stones and charging the giant. Your giant is controlling your life and not taking action is only giving the giant more control.
- Finish the job. Once Goliath went down by the stone, there was still his head to cut off. When facing your giant, do not think that it is over just because it looks like you won the battle. Do not stop taking your medication because it's a "good day." Do not take your marriage for granted just because you're not fighting. Keep working hard at work to show that you are valuable and the company would be lost without you. Keep talking to your kids even when you think they are not listening.
- Trust God. David had been prepared as a shepherd fighting animals that wanted his sheep. Think back to all God has done for you preparing for the battles that lie ahead. You are one of God's children and He will not leave you to perish. Call out to Him, trust Him with all your being and have the confidence that you walk with God in all your battles.

We need to look at giants in our life differently. David versus Goliath is not a story about a young lad against a large man. It is a battle of God-focus versus self-focus. When Saul focused on the Philistine's he stumbled and became scared. When David focused on Saul chasing him, he lied, ran away and hid. When David focused on God, he defeated Goliath and his outlook with Saul was much different. The giants fall when you focus on God.

Psalm 27:1-5 The LORD is my light and my salvation—so why should I be afraid? The LORD is my fortress, protecting me from danger, so why should I tremble? When evil people come to devour me, when my enemies and foes attack me, they will stumble and fall. Though a mighty army surrounds me, my heart will not be afraid. Even if I am attacked, I will remain confident. The one thing I ask of the LORD—the thing I seek most—is to live in the house of the LORD all the days of my life, delighting in the LORD's perfections and meditating in his Temple. For he will conceal me there when troubles come; he will hide me in his sanctuary. He will place me out of reach on a high rock.

As we wrap up this chapter, I wanted to end with a part of the David versus Goliath story that is often overlooked. David is preparing to go into battle against Goliath when these series of events occur:

*1 Samuel 17:38-40 Then Saul dressed David in his own tunic. He put a coat of armor on him and a bronze helmet on his head. David fastened on his sword over the tunic and tried walking around, because he was not used to them. "I cannot go in these, "he said to Saul, "because I am not used to them." So he took them off. Then he took his staff in his hand, chose **five smooth stones** from the stream, put them in the pouch of his shepherd's bag and, with his sling in his hand, approached the Philistine. (bold my emphasis)*

Did David doubt his abilities and need five stones in case he missed? No, Goliath had brothers and David was prepared in case they decided to help. David did not need armor, a sword or a shield. He was armed with the confidence that God had provided and all the weapons he needed to take down this giant, a stone and slingshot.

Max Lucado notes that the five stones are symbolic for us when looking to conquer the giants in our life. His book, Facing Your Giants, is a great read and highly recommended.

1) Stone of the past—remember all the victories God has provided you.
2) Stone of prayer—prayer is what spawned all of David's successes.
3) Stone of priority—highest priority is God's reputation; are you willing to give your life of God?
4) Stone of passion—run towards your giant with the passion that they will be defeated.
5) Stone of persistence—never give up fighting and praying; God can overcome all giants.

Personal Application

We all will face giants in our life and Steve and Ruth have not been immune just because of their Christian faith. They are both able to identify those "giants" in their life that resulted in a deeper relationship with God and proved to be another part of the maturation process. Here are a few of their thoughts:

- Experiencing a giant can sometimes take you through the stages of grief, often times finding the giant hard to accept for a long time.
- Sense of loss almost always accompanies a giant but it's important to step back and see if God is reprioritizing what and where He wants you.
- Recognize the limitations that the giant has on you at the time and pray for strength, guidance, wisdom to overcome.
- Sometimes the giant allows you the opportunity and freedom to become involved in different activities that you were restricted from doing before.
- Working through the giant is an opportunity to be God's hands and realize that this struggle may be part of the process of God "plowing the field" for the work to be done.
- If there is a giant that includes others being defiant and disobedient to God's word and plan then God will discipline them; it is not our job to do so.
- Overcoming the giant leaves you with a sense of awe in what God can do.

SIN

Romans 7:21-25 So I find this law at work: When I want to do good, evil is right there with me. For in my inner being I delight in God's law; but I see another law at work in the members of my body, waging war against the law of my mind and making me a prisoner of the law of sin at work within my members. What a wretched man I am! Who will rescue me from this body of death? Thanks, be to God—through Jesus Christ our Lord! So then, I myself in my mind am a slave to God's law, but in the sinful nature a slave to the law of sin.

I absolutely dread writing this chapter for many reasons. One reason is because of how harsh God speaks about sin. There is no way to sugar coat how God feels about sin:

Romans 6:23a For the wages of sin is death

God hates sin so much that He needed to send His son, Jesus, to pay the price for our sins. That's the second reason why this is hard to write and think about: Jesus had to come from heaven, lead a perfect, sinless life and then suffer more than anyone ever has just because I choose to be selfish and sinful. The third reason why this is difficult is that it causes me to take a hard look at the sin in my life. I wish I could say that the sin stopped when I was saved but that's not what happened. There have been changes made in my sin life but the biggest change is how much more aware I've become when I sin and the disappointment I bring to God because I should know better.

Sin has a predictable pattern:

1) We ignore or move away from God's truth
2) We replace God with something or someone else (a friend refers to this as a "new shiny")
3) If or when we stay in our sin, we reject God.

If we stay in our sin long enough and reject God, He will give us over to the sin and the consequences that come.

But here's a funny thing regarding humans and sin. We want, at times demand, that God deal with others sin quickly and harshly. In our minds, we have already judged the individual and determined their punishment, now we just need God to act. Yet, how do we look at our own sin? Are we grateful that God is not that way with us? We want God to be kind, tolerant and patient while we work through our sinful ways and "come back" to Him.

When we are right with God, we should trust His plan. We need to trust that God knows the truth about everything and He will deal with sin. But remember, God's judgment will be fair in His eyes, not according to us. If we confess these sins and ask for forgiveness, and turn away from the sin, then we will experience the freedom that God offers through grace.

By being in relationship with God as believers, we know we are forgiven and have that peace and security. However, non believers will experience guilt and uncertainty while struggling in their sin. I am not saying that believers will not struggle with guilt when sin occurs but you can feel confident knowing there is forgiveness because of your faith. Remember, it is God's kindness that can turn someone from sin and lead to repentance.

> *Romans 2:3-4 So when you, a mere man, pass judgment on them and yet do the same things, do you think you will escape God's judgment? Or do you show contempt for the riches of his kindness, tolerance and patience, not realizing that God's kindness leads you toward repentance?*

God's kindness invites us to change by sending the right words at the right time to encourage change. God sends the right person into our life to encourage change; to walk along side us when we need them most. If we are accepting then we listen and begin the change process. If we are not open, then these words and people are seen as intrusions and rejected.

I've worked with many individuals who claim that their intentions were good and they want to do good but they can't help sinning.

Romans 2:6-13 God "will give to each person according to what he has done." To those who by persistence in doing good seek glory, honor and immortality, he will give eternal life. But for those who are self-seeking and who reject the truth and follow evil, there will be wrath and anger. There will be trouble and distress for every human being who does evil: first for the Jew, then for the Gentile; but glory, honor and peace for everyone who does good: first for the Jew, then for the Gentile. For God does not show favoritism. All who sin apart from the law will also perish apart from the law, and all who sin under the law will be judged by the law. For it is not those who hear the law who are righteous in god's sight, but it is those who obey the law who will be declared righteous.

God will judge us by our actions. Don't misunderstand: He knows our hearts desire but when we are right with God we want to do right and we will do right. We do not claim to have a deep, personal relationship with God and then go out and sin repeatedly.

Now the great news for us sinners is found in Romans 2:16:

This will take place on the day when God will judge men's secrets through Jesus Christ

See, when you belong to God and believe that Jesus paid the price for your sins, then the forgiveness that He offers for our sins will be received. For nonbelievers, God will deal with sin apart from Jesus as He claims, "I do not know you."

Matthew 10:32-33 "Whoever acknowledges me before men, I will also acknowledge him before my Father in heaven. But whoever disowns me before men, I will disown him before my Father in heaven."

Picture standing before God as He reviews your life's actions and thoughts with two options: Jesus stands up and says, "I already paid the price for those" or Jesus claims He does not know you. You can feel joy, elation and thankfulness or alone, fearful and filled with regret.

Stopping sinful behavior is not always easy. Sin can create very <u>temporary</u> pleasurable emotions but they are only temporary.

> *Hebrews 11:24-26 By faith Moses, when he had grown up, refused to be known as the son of Pharaoh's daughter. He chose to be mistreated along with the people of God rather than to enjoy the pleasures of sin for a short time. He regarded disgrace for the sake of Christ as of greater value than the treasures of Egypt, because he was looking ahead to his reward.*

The emotional consequences that follow sin are certainly not fun and not something I would wish on anyone but those consequences are necessary. That is God's Spirit teaching us right from wrong and correcting our behavior. The good news is that you have these consequences because you have a relationship with God. This also means that the price for your sin has been paid through the blood of Jesus. You want to overcome sin? Try these steps:

- *Acknowledge the sin:* stop trying to deny that it does not exist – you are only trying to fooling yourself and my guess is that you are not doing a very good job of that.
- *Pray to God:* get in a quiet place with no distractions and have a conversation with your Father regarding your behavior. He already knows what you have done but He wants you to bring it to Him and confess the sin.
- *Accept God's forgiveness:* be willing to accept God's grace and mercy. But here's the big step, if you truly accept God's forgiveness then you need to forgive yourself and let it go. Many people will claim God's forgiveness and then hold on to the guilt. If God has forgiven you then you need to forgive yourself otherwise you do not truly believe you have been forgiven.
- *Go, and sin no more:* Once you have acknowledged your sin, prayed and confessed to God, accepted His forgiveness the final step is to go, and sin no more. Read this passage about sin:

John 8:1-11: But Jesus went to the Mount of Olives. At dawn he appeared again in the temple courts, where all the people gathered around him, and he sat down to teach them. The teachers of the law and the Pharisees brought in a woman caught in adultery. They made her stand before the group and said to Jesus, "Teacher, this woman was caught in the act of adultery. In the Law Moses commanded us to stone such women. Now what do you say?" They were using this question as a trap, in order to have a basis for accusing him. But Jesus bent down and started to write on the ground with his finger. When they kept on questioning him, he straightened up and said to them, "If any one of you is without sin, let him be the first to throw a stone at her." Again he stooped down and wrote on the ground. At this, those who heard began to go away one at a time, the older ones first, until only Jesus was left, with the woman still standing there. Jesus straightened up and asked her, "Woman, where are they? Has no one condemned you?" "No one, sir," she said. "Then neither do I condemn you," Jesus declared. "Go now and leave your life of sin."

What happens when you have worked through the sinful act, completed the steps above and claimed forgiveness then you sin again? Repeat the above steps knowing that each time there is a maturity in you growing and deepening. Do not lose hope, know that God is always available and wants to talk to you, especially about your sin.

I have had the opportunity to speak with many individuals who state that the temptation to sin is too strong and that God is tempting them to sin. James speaks very clearly regarding the process of sin:

James 1:13-15 When tempted, no one should say, "God is tempting me." For God cannot be tempted by evil, nor does he tempt anyone; but each one is tempted when, by his own evil desire, he is dragged away and enticed. Then, after desire has conceived, it gives birth to sin; and sin, when it is full-grown, gives birth to death.

When tempted, no one should say, "God is tempting me." God is not tempting us but instead we walk to sin because of our own selfish desires.

For those who like to see equations, try this:

Our evil desire (temptation) ⇨ Sin ⇨ Death

God will not tempt you. God will not contradict Himself. He is not going to say "keep the marriage bed pure" as He does in Hebrews 13 and then turn around and say sleep with whomever you want.

If we look just a few verses earlier in James, we see what happens when we overcome trials:

James 1:12 Blessed is the man who perseveres under trial, because when he has stood the test, he will receive the crown of life that God has promised to those who love him.

All of this brings me back to the question of, what if we know God's word, know what we are suppose to do and yet we still sin? God's word is pretty clear on this and the reaction should be enough to make us all never sin again.

We are going to look at a few passages in Hebrews and 2 Peter regarding this question. Remember, the question is, what if we know better and still sin?

In Hebrews 10, this question is specifically answered:

Hebrews 10:26-31 If we deliberately keep on sinning after we have received the knowledge of the truth, no sacrifice for sins is left, but only a fearful expectation of judgment and of raging fire that will consume the enemies of God. Anyone who rejected the law of Moses died without mercy on the testimony of two or three witnesses. How much more severely do you think a man deserves to be punished who has trampled the Son of God under foot, who has treated as an unholy thing the blood of the covenant that sanctified him, and who has insulted the Sprit of grace? For we know him who said,

"It is mine to avenge; I will repay," and again, "The Lord will judge his people." It is a dreadful thing to fall into the hands of the living God.

The writer of Hebrews tells us that if we keep on sinning after we know the truth then we deserve to be punished severely because we are treating Jesus' sacrifice as unholy and should expect a fearful judgment. Again, we should now better as Christians than to keep sinning because the truth has been revealed to us.

If that isn't clear enough then 2 Peter really drives home the point! In 2 Peter 2, Peter is talking about false teachers but look at the themes and words used in these verses:

2 Peter 10: This is especially true of those who follow the corrupt desire of the sinful nature and despise authority.

2 Peter 14: With eyes full of adultery, they never stop sinning; they seduce the unstable; they are experts in greed

2 Peter 18: For the mouth empty, boastful words and, by appealing to the lustful desires of sinful human nature, the entice people who are just escaping from those who live in error.

2 Peter 19: They promise them freedom, while they themselves are slaves of depravity—for a man is a slave to whatever has mastered him.

But the most powerful verses are 20 and 21:

2 Peter 2:20-21: If they have escaped the corruption of the world by knowing our Lord and Savior Jesus Christ and are again entangled in it and overcome, they are worse off at the end than they were at the beginning. It would have been better for them not to have known the way of righteousness, than to have known it and then to turn their backs on the sacred command that was passed on to them.

If you know the Lord, His word, His desire for you and knowingly walk away it would have been much better for you to never have known about righteousness.

But this is not a chapter of all doom and gloom, in fact this is where Jesus and His shed blood shine the most! Look back at the passage in John 8:1-11 which provides the healing, forgiving story of Jesus and sin and focus on verse 11.

> *John 8:10-11 Jesus straightened up and asked her, "Woman, where are they? Has no one condemned you?" "No one, sir," she said. "Then neither do I condemn you," Jesus declared. "Go now and leave your life of sin."*

The adulterer is not condemned by Jesus, but is told to go and sin no more. If you are stuck in the rut of sin, sin that you know better than to be in then cease, end the sin right now, confess to God and receive His healing and forgiveness. No sin is too great that cannot be forgiven but you cannot expect to knowingly stay in sin without there being serious consequences, even if those consequences don't come until you meet God face to face.

If this feels completely overwhelming to you, consider Christian counseling where you can receive help ending this pattern and seeing where forgiveness lies for you. Sin is the most destructive thing that can happen to us because it separates us from God but we don't have to stay there. Let's do everything we can to restore that relationship and enjoy being God's children.

Personal application

For the application to this chapter, I asked Steve and Ruth for their lessons learned/ encouragement for Christians, especially who might be newer to their faith, when they are faced with sin in their life.

- Several things come to mind. First, we categorize sin as some worse than others but in God's sight, a half truth is just as bad as murder or abortion, or anything else we can think. It all caused Jesus to have to go to the cross.
- Then I remember in Hebrews 12 where the writer tells us to strip off the sin that so easily hinders our progress as Christians.

- King David also says in the Psalms that if he has sin in his heart God won't hear him which tells us that sin breaks the fellowship with God. He won't listen to us except when we ask for forgiveness.
- When we feel like our prayers are "bouncing off the ceiling" we need to ask God to show us if there is sin in our lives. That may not be the case but I believe that is a problem in many of us.
- God's word also reminds us that God is quick to forgive and never remembers our sins again.
- There is forgiveness and He restores our fellowship with Him. What an AWESOME God we have!

DOUBT

John 20:25 "Unless I see...I will not believe."

Luke 7:19 "Are you the Expected One, or do we look for someone else?"

Doubt is to question whether something is real or exist. I'm sure there are many examples of things you have doubted, including God. Did you know that biblically there were followers of Jesus who doubted? Most are familiar with the apostle Thomas who doubted that Jesus had risen from the grave until he saw Jesus' scared hands and side: see John 20:25. But did you know there was another prominent character who doubted? Read the passage of Luke 7 to see the doubt that John the Baptist experienced regarding Jesus.

Luke 7:18-28 John's disciples told him about all these things. Calling two of them, he sent them to the Lord to ask, "Are you the one who was to come, or should we expect someone else?" When the men came to Jesus, they said, "John the Baptist sent us to you to ask, 'Are you the one who was to come, or should we expect someone else?'" At that very time Jesus cured many who had diseases, sicknesses and evil spirits and gave sight to many who were blind. So he replied to the messengers, "Go back and report to John what you have seen and heard: The blind receive sight, the lame walk, those who have leprosy are cured, the deaf hear, the dead are raised, and the good news is preached to the poor. Blessed is the man who does not fall away on account of me." After John's messengers left, Jesus began to speak to the crowd about John: "What did you go out into the desert to see? A reed swayed by the wind? If not, what did you go out to see? A man dressed in fine clothes? No, those who wear expensive clothes and indulge in luxury are in palaces. But what did you go out to see? A prophet? Yes, I tell you, and more than a prophet. This is the one about whom it is written: "'I will send my messenger ahead of you, who will prepare your way before you.' I tell you, among those born of women there is no one greater that John; yet the one who is least in the kingdom of God is greater than he."

Why would John the Baptist doubt that Jesus is who he said he was? Where was John the Baptist when he sent his messengers to Jesus? We have to go back a few chapters for that answer.

Luke 3:15-20 The people were waiting expectantly and were all wondering in their hearts if John might possibly be the Christ. John answered them all, "I baptize you with water. But one more powerful than I will come, the thongs of whose sandals I am not worthy to untie. He will baptize you with the Holy Spirit and with fire. His winnowing fork is in his hand to clear his threshing floor and to gather the wheat into his barn, but he will burn up the chaff with unquenchable fire." And with many other words John exhorted the people and preached the good news to them. But when John rebuked Herod the tetrarch because of Herodias, his brother's wife, and all the other evil things he had done, Herod added this to them all: He locked John up in prison.

You may be saying to yourself that there is no way that John the Baptist doubted. Sure he was odd, living in the desert, eating locusts and honey but he was a prophet, he preached Jesus coming, he baptized Jesus and was present when God spoke from Heaven (Matt 3:17). Yet, he did doubt that Jesus was who said he was.

To understand John the Baptist doubt, you must understand where he was at the moment. John was in prison; he was unsure of his future yet he knew he did not deserve to be there. John wanted out of prison and probably began to wonder whether Jesus would or could save him.

So, John questioned what he already knew about Jesus. He sent messengers to Jesus to inquire if he knew John was in prison and if he was the messiah or should they expect someone else. I think John thought, "surely Jesus would free me from this prison if he just knew I was here!" John struggled with the thought that Jesus, the Messiah, the King of the World would turn his back on a faithful prophet.

He goes through a brief period of doubting because Jesus was not responding the way John wanted him. This happens to us as well. We think that God should respond a certain way and when He does not, we start to doubt God's plan, His will, does He know our circumstances, does He hear us and sometimes, does He even exist.

When you doubt something, did you know that you already have an opinion on the matter? Have you doubted that you are smart, pretty, tall, thin, young, old or good enough? Have you doubted whether God can use you because of your past? Have you doubted whether God can answer your prayer, show you His will for your life or even exist?

Doubt comes when we try to put God in a box. Thomas and the other disciples struggled with the death of Jesus. They believed that Jesus was King but they wanted the kingdom established right then and as they wanted. They were not interested in a heavenly kingdom, they wanted an earthly kingdom and believed that Jesus would gather his army, destroy the Romans and they would rule with Him on earth. They were in disbelief when He was crucified and placed in the tomb. There was no rejoicing that a savior had just given his life and paid the price for our sins. For three long, agonizing days the disciples grieved and doubted what had happened the last three years with Jesus.

But, Jesus rose!

John 20:19-21 That Sunday evening the disciples were meeting behind locked doors because they were afraid of the Jewish leaders. Suddenly, Jesus was standing there among them! "Peace be with you," he said. As he spoke, he showed them the wounds in his hands and his side. They were filled with joy when they saw the Lord! Again he said, "Peace be with you. As the Father has sent me, so I am sending you."

Now the disciples were excited, energized, filled with hope and there was no more doubt. But Thomas was so consumed by his disbelief and doubt that he was not with the others. Even when the disciples found Thomas and shared the great news, Thomas did not believe. It was not until Thomas was able to see and feel Jesus' hands and side that he believed Jesus was alive.

What happens when we feel this way? We have all doubted things but what happens when we doubt God? This is really our response to how we think God should respond. God has given us many examples of individuals that were faced with horrible circumstances yet remained faithful and trusting in God: see Joseph, Hosea, Paul and Job. We are going to experience times when our family does not act the way we think they should. Our marriages will not always be a bed of roses, there will be fights, your spouse might even walk away. What happens when you lose a job, your home a child dies; where will you turn?

For years, I have worked with individuals and families that have experienced all these and more. The individuals who know God and have walked with Him are much better prepared when crisis and doubt strikes. Don't misunderstand: believers can and do get mad at God. There are stages that we all experience when crisis occurs that include shock, denial, anger and eventually acceptance. There is not a timetable for how long one stays in each stage and everyone who experiences a crisis reacts differently. But, if your foundation is in the relationship you have with God and you trust the will He has for you, his grace and mercy will sustain you.

Chuck Swindoll, who has been a great inspiration in this chapter, talks about three practical things to remember when you find yourself doubting. The first is that God cannot lie. He will test us, will sometimes say no, yes or wait but He will never lie. Do not be led by doubt that tries to convince you that God would not put you through your current crisis.

The second perspective is that we will not lose. God has His own timing and purpose and although we do not always understand the meaning we can trust that God prevails and defeats evil and sin. Therefore, we that believe in Him will be delivered through any trial or doubt.

The third thing to remember is that Jesus does not leave. Jesus will always be with, fight for and deliver us. This does not promise great health, financial security, well behaved children or a great marriage but it does mean that we will be in his presence for eternity.

Personal Application

To begin the discussion on doubt, Steve and Ruth were asked to talk about a time when they struggled with their faith or knowing God's will. Ruth was able to relate a time regarding a serious health issue where she struggled with not feeling peace and joy and was desperate to find God during the trial. Steve shared of a time during college, as we know many struggle during this time. Intimate relationships, difficult courses, financial concerns and being away from home can cause a great deal of doubt for everyone, including a Christian. Here are additional thoughts from them when that season of doubt occurs:

- Feeling of wanting to know that God is real especially when we hurt.
- Struggling with God's timeline compared to our timeline.
- During pain and doubt that there is a deeper hunger for God. It is during these times that the relationship intensifies and becomes much more personal.
- Just because you attend church and life groups regularly, when you are hurting and doubting you often are just going through the motions.
- The struggle to find God even when you feel that you are working the plan that God has laid out for you.
- The reality of feeling God wrap you up in a "warm blanket" to comfort us when we finally focus on Him and surrender.
- The relief upon realizing that God is there has heard our prayers and healing begins.

FIGHTING EVIL

Ephesians 6:12 – For our struggle is not against flesh and blood, but against the rulers, against the authorities, against the powers of this dark world and against the spiritual forces of evil in the heavenly realms.

Here's how one individual described his battle with evil: For a long time, I spent all my time, energy and focus struggling. The battle being fought was a no win situation. I struggled with competition, greed, lust – always feeling like what I was doing was not enough or not good enough. I still struggle with those occasionally but once I realized who the real fight was with, my outlook and tactics changed.

I imagine many of you can relate to this description as you battle some form of evil. We struggle, we think we've won and then here comes another battle that often includes anger, frustration, disappointment and being tired from the constant fight and little relief. If you are stuck in the struggle, as we all have been, two things stick out for me: 1) it's time to grow our maturity in faith; 2) Satan wants to win and will do anything to do so.

Let's look back at Ephesians 6:12. It very clearly tells us that we are not battling each other; we are at war with Satan and the powers of the dark world. Here is where our maturity needs to occur. As a Christian you have to realize and recognize that Satan is real and there are evil spiritual forces that want to cause you and I to sin and turn from God.

Isaiah 14:12-15 – How you have fallen from heaven, O morning star, son of the dawn! You have been cast down to the earth, you who once laid low the nations! You said in your heart, "I will ascend to heaven; I will raise my throne above the stars of God; I will sit enthroned on the mount of assembly, on the utmost heights of the sacred mountain. I will ascend above the tops of the clouds; I will make myself like the Most High." But you are brought down to the grave, to the depths of the pit.

This may be difficult for you to always remember because we do not see Satan in person or the evil spirits but you experience them constantly. This takes maturity on our part to recognize evil and realize that we cannot fight the battle by ourselves because we will lose every time. Now, if you have the maturity to realize and recognize Satan and evil you have the maturity to know how to fight evil and win.

Ephesians 6:13 – Therefore put on the full armor of God, so that when the day of evil comes, you may be able to stand your ground, and after you have done everything, to stand.

If you read this literally you are looking for steel armor to put on so that you are protected but let's not look literal as much as spiritual in what we are instructed to do. This verse is telling us that God fights evil and He has provided all the tools necessary for us to be victorious in this fight.

Ephesians 6:14a – Stand firm then, with the belt of truth buckled around your waist,

Do you know the truth? Satan does, he knows the whole history of the Bible, of the role Jesus plays and knows the plan is for Jesus to return and establish His kingdom. However, Satan wants to change the plan. He is egotistical and believes he is more powerful than God and one of the ways he likes to try and prove this is by turning Christians to sin and away from our Creator. Knowing the truth sets us free from the bondage of sin and gives no power to Satan.

Ephesians 6:14b – with the breastplate of righteousness in place.

God has made us righteous when we repent. Therefore, there should not be any ongoing sin in our life. If there is, it needs to be repented and confessed to God so that our righteousness can be restored. Without righteousness provided, we are extremely vulnerable to maintain in our sinful pattern and give Satan a better opportunity to influence us.

> *Ephesians 6:15 – with your feet fitted with the readiness that comes from the gospel of peace.*

What happens to you when there is anger, resentment, greed, lust and other selfish feelings? Are you more apt to be quick to disrupt peace? When you promote peace, you are promoting harmony from God to God's people. When you have peace and you are prepared to keep the peace, Satan cannot divide or separate you from others.

> *Ephesians 6:16 – In addition to all this, take up the shield of faith, with which you can extinguish all the flaming arrows of the evil one.*

Without faith, you can do nothing for God. Faith is what drives us and promotes a desire in us to do good and live for Jesus. You are going to have faith in something: either God and know that Jesus died and rose again for you or yourself who can be very tempted by Satan and evil desires. Our faith in God will give us the strength to resist and fight the evil temptations.

> *Ephesians 6:17 – Take the helmet of salvation and the sword of the Spirit, which is the word of God.*

We need to know that our salvation is secure. Jesus died one time to save us and while we still sin, we cannot lose our salvation nor have it taken from us. Knowing this gives us the confidence to stand firm but we also need to know God's word. When you are tempted do you know the word of God to be able to comfort you, provide strength and rid Satan who is trying to tempt you? I'm sure we all need to do a better job of knowing the Bible and how it can help us.

> *Ephesians 6:18 – And pray in the spirit on all occasions with all kinds of prayers and requests. With this in mind, be alert and always keep on praying for all the saints.*

Prayer. How is that prayer life going for you? Is it a constant, open dialogue with God or maybe just when you are in trouble and need something? Prayer is our direct link to God where we can tell Him everything and He can and does respond to us. If we do not have an open communication with God where we can share our joy, hurts, frustrations, temptations, then Satan has the opportunity to start filling our head and that is never a good idea. If it has been awhile since you really prayed, may I suggest you hit your knees and start a conversation; God is waiting for you.

Fighting and defeating evil is not going to be easy. However, God told us in Ephesians how to overcome and be prepared. Follow these steps and see the difference it makes next time the dark world comes after you.

Personal application

Satan is constantly battling to separate us from God. For Steve and Ruth I wanted to know what would be their guidance or words of encouragement for someone during those times that evil is hitting hard.

- When the world around me seems so out of control and there is so much hate, violence and pain, I remember what Paul says in Ephesians that we are not fighting people but it is spiritual warfare all around.
- The enemy is real and very strong and is using people to fight against God.
- It is so easy to be fearful of what the future holds but then I go back to what God says in His word. Over and over especially in the Psalms, the writers tell us not to "fret" because of the evil doers. They will be held accountable for their deeds.
- He is a God of justice and He sees everything that is happening.
- WE are told to put on God's armor and that includes salvation, truth, righteous living and using the sword which is His word and staying in prayer.
- We cannot face the evil around us without spending time reading His word and praying. He encourages us through His word and praying helps us to focus on <u>Who</u> He is and that we belong to Almighty God.

GRACE

Romans 6:11 so you also should consider yourselves to be dead to the power of sin and alive to God through Christ Jesus.

Romans 6:16 don't you realize that you become the slave of whatever you choose to obey? You can be a slave to sin, which leads to death, or you can choose to obey God, which leads to righteous living.

Where would we be without grace? Grace is a wonderful, precious gift from God where he can demonstrate His true love for us. Grace is what allows us to stand before God after a life filled with sin. Remember, it is our sin that has separated us from God and only grace can restore our hope and eternal life.

Chuck Swindoll has written a great book, The Grace Awakening Devotional, and has a series of daily devotionals on grace that are excellent resources. Pastor Swindoll talks about how receiving God's grace does not mean that we have stopped sinning, that we have been made righteous or that we have become perfect. What grace does is declares us righteous before God.

When we, as a sinner, accept this gift a few things happen that we will discuss because I don't know that most Christians understand the terms: repentance, justification, sanctification.

Repentance: Change your mind toward Christ and accept grace as a free gift, acknowledging there is nothing you did to deserve the gift.

Justification: God declares us righteous through our faith. This does not make us perfect, means that God declared us righteous in His eyes.

Sanctification: Now that we have been justified, we begin a process of growing mature in our faith. As sanctification occurs we find ourselves wanting to sin less because we want to honor Christ.

The great thing about this process is that God provides the grace while we are still in our sin. Sanctification does not happen overnight and yet God is continuing to grow us and move us to be more like Jesus. It helps me to think of this as freedom. This is not freedom to sin all I want because I know I'm saved. It's a freedom to know that I can choose <u>not</u> to sin. It's a freedom from guilt knowing that when I do sin, as we all will continue to do, that I'm saved for eternity because God justified me. It's freedom to move in a direction that pleases my Heavenly Father and become more mature in all areas.

Another large freedom I now possess is from other people. Let me explain because this is a big issue within our society and continues to intensify. Many may call this legalism but I want to define it even clearer. We have a problem in this world where everyone believes it is okay to voice and attempt to enforce their opinion. Having an opinion is great but that does not mean that your opinion is accurate especially for me. When someone tries to claim that they are a "good person" and therefore will go to Heaven or claim that they do not commit the "big" sins so everything is good, they are fooling themselves. These beliefs and the ensuing attempts to manipulate by being prideful or create guilt and shame is what we can claim freedom from. Our motivation becomes pleasing God and thanking Him for providing grace while we still sin.

What becomes sad to see is when proclaimed Christians feel so bogged down in their faith that there is no joy in them. God wants us to have fun and not be tied down by what we should not be or should not do. Many of non-Christians views about faith and God come from watching Christians and the church. Are you living a life that is happy and cheerful because of what God has done or is there no difference in the way you behave from a non-believer? Is your church sharing a message of joy and hope or is it so focused on what you cannot do that you feel like you will never be good enough to measure up? We have freedom from all this because God is who we answer and He already says, "come on in to the family, it does not matter what you did or will do, your mine." Knowing that once you have made this choice, you want to continue to grow in faith and listening to others trying to impose their thoughts on you has no place anymore. Stop thinking you have to please someone else in order to follow God. As Paul told the Galatians:

Galatians 5:7 you were running, well; who hindered you from obeying the truth?

Let's take a look at how you can further claim freedom because in order to have this freedom you need to understand what Jesus did for you. In Romans 6, Paul is talking about how grace has overcome sin's power. Paul focuses a great deal on "knowing" that we, our old, sinful self was crucified with Jesus. Now this is a hard concept for many and one I struggled for a long time because I was not there when Jesus was crucified so how can this happen? It's important to realize that we do not think the same way God does. If we try to use our logic to comprehend what Jesus did for us then we will always struggle with this concept. So, stop trying to be so analytical and realize that God has supernatural powers. When Jesus was crucified, He paid the price for all sin that has ever occurred. Sin before His crucifixion and after. Only Jesus could do this and therefore when the Bible says you were baptized into His death and crucified with Him, there is a leap of faith that you need to take, even, especially if you do not understand it all.

It was for freedom that Christ set us free.

Galatians 5:1 So Christ has truly set us free. Now make sure that you stay free, and don't get tied up again in slavery to the law.

In the movie, The Matrix, Morpheus gives Neo a choice: take the blue pill and go back to the life you know or take the red pill and be free to know the truth. Neo takes the red pill and thus begins a long journey of experiencing the price to be free. Grace does not constrain us; it frees us from sin, to grow. Check out these verses regarding the freedom that Jesus has provided:

Romans 6:7 For he who has died is freed from sin.

Romans 8:2 For the law of the Spirit of life in Christ Jesus has set you free.

Romans 8:28-32 And we know that in all things God works for the good of those who love him, who have been called according to his purpose. For those God foreknew he also predestined to be conformed to the likeness of his Son, that he might be the firstborn among many brothers. And those he predestined, he also called; those he called, he also justified; those he justified, he also glorified. What, then, shall we say in response to this? If God is for us, who can be against us? He who did not spare his own Son, but gave him up for us all—how will he not also, along with him, graciously give us all things?

John 8:36 So if the Son makes you free, you will be free indeed.

How wonderful this freedom is! Our Lord and Savior, Jesus, paid the price for our sins not only for eternity to be with Him, but so that we could experience grace and freedom on Earth. And in doing so, we have the great opportunity to show grace to others. We do this by encouraging and building up, not providing certain rules or guidelines they need to fit into as defined by us. We have been given the option of choice: walk with God and enjoy all the blessings and strength he offers or walk on our own and experience the consequences that will surely follow. But remember that when we walk our own way, we also have the choice to walk back to God and find forgiveness; however the consequences of sin may stay with you forever.

Remember, this choice that you have been given must also be given to others. None of us are perfect and therefore cannot tell others the perfect formula to remain free from sin. If you are trying to control someone and make grace conditional then stop. Let your spouse, children and friends grow and experience God's grace. Yes they may fail sometimes but how sweet will it be to watch them succeed!

Let's take a look at what a few other verses say about grace:

Romans 6:15-18 What then? Shall we sin because we are not under law but under grace? By no means! Don't you know that when you offer yourselves to someone to obey him as slaves, you are slaves to the one whom you obey—whether you are slaves to sin, which leads to death, or to obedience, which leads to righteousness? But thanks be to God that, though you used to be slaves to sin, you wholeheartedly obeyed the form of teaching to which you were entrusted. You have been set free from sin and have become slaves to righteousness.

Even while we are free we still will be slaves to something. Will it be a master that is bad for us like money, drugs, sex, greed or control? Or, would you rather be in a relationship with God where righteousness can occur? There are only these two choices but we have been given the freedom to choose a path.

Psalm 85:2 You forgave the iniquity of your people and covered all their sins.

God forgave our sins and guilt. Are you showing that same grace to others or do they feel more guilt because of you?

Chuck Swindoll pulls four guidelines out of Romans 14 when we talk about providing grace to others. To set the stage for these guidelines, here are a few verses from Paul:

Romans 14:4, 7-13, 19, 22 Who are you to judge someone else's servant? To his own master he stands or falls. And he will stand, for the Lord is able to make him stand. For none of us lives to himself alone and none of us dies to himself alone. If we live, we live to the Lord; and if we die, we die to the Lord. So, whether we live or die, we belong to the Lord. For this very reason, Christ died and returned to life so that he might be the Lord of both the dead and the living. You, then, why do you judge your brother? Or why do you look down on your brother? For we will all stand before God's judgment seat. It is written: "'As surely as I live,' says the Lord, 'every knee will bow before me; every tongue will confess to God.'" So then, each of us will give an account of himself to God. Therefore let us stop passing judgment on one another. Instead, make up your mind not to put any stumbling block or obstacle in your brother's way. Let us therefore make every effort to do what leads to peace and to mutual edification. So whatever you believe about these things keep between yourself and God. Blessed is the man who does not condemn himself by what he approves.

To summarize Pastor Swindoll's points:

1) <u>You must accept others in order to let them be</u>. Accept others without putting conditions on them.
2) <u>If you refuse to dictate how others should live, God can have a greater impact in their lives</u>. Each one of us needs to choose our own path. This is hopefully the path laid out by God and not you. You can be supportive but do not hold someone back because they are not walking the same path you would like.
3) <u>Releasing others means we do not fill a position we are not qualified to hold</u>. We jump to many conclusions that we should not. Therefore, if we release them we do not judge.
4) <u>Loving others means giving liberty wisely</u>. Who are we trying to please? It should be God so don't make someone have you as the object they should please. Live your life for Christ, not anyone else.

You may be thinking at this point that you've got it, I need to show grace to everyone. But what if you have a disagreement with someone who is a fellow Christian. What if they do not believe the same as you on biblical issues? It is a fact that Christians will disagree and sometimes on very big issues.

There are many out there who take a hard stance and believe their way is the only way. While you may be right on the issue to a certain degree, the meat of the issue gets lost because of your personality and delivery style. Have you ever been in an argument or disagreement and at some point you are arguing about something completely different? There is an art to "disagreement" and it always includes respect for the other party and maintaining focus on the issue. Remember, the other person's side is just as valid and important as yours so listen openly to what they have to say. You might just learn something but you will definitely be showing grace.

As we wrap up grace, there are a few keys to always keep in mind:

- Grace is available to everyone who comes to the Lord and we will be coming many times before Him asking for grace. This is a long process that requires time and will be painful but is so desperately needed.
- God's grace releases us from sin and the shame associated with our sin. Be very thankful for this freedom, share your freedom with others and let go of the guilt. You are free, start acting like it!
- Show grace to others. At work, at home and in your community, show grace. Teach others and be a model. They say kids are always watching their parent's behavior but we all are always watching others. Be the model.
- Grace starts with repentance, moves to justification and then the process of sanctification begins. There is no limit as to the number of times you can come and repent to God.

We'll close with Paul's words to the Ephesians:

Ephesians 6:23-24 Peace to the brothers, and love with faith from God the Father and the Lord Jesus Christ. Grace to all who love our Lord Jesus Christ with an undying love.

Personal application

Grace is such a wonderful gift and I wanted Steve and Ruth to share some of the ways that grace has impacted how they live and treat others?

- What an Awesome concept, Grace! I think about it every single day. His grace is what gets me through life.
- I love the verse in Hebrews 4:16 where we are told that we can come to God's throne any time and in any circumstance and ask for His grace to help us through whatever happening. To me, that means that no matter what is going on, He will give me just what I need: patience, wisdom, understanding, love or anything else that is needed.

- It reminds me that Almighty God cares about what is going on my life and that I don't have to be afraid of what is coming down the road because He is able and willing to supply all my needs as Paul says in Philippians.

HUMILITY

Romans 12:3 For by the grace given me I say to every one of you: do not think of yourself more highly than you ought, but rather think of yourself with sober judgment, in accordance with the measure of faith God has given you.

We have many different examples in our world of individuals or groups who think much higher of themselves than they should. Check out the athletes, Hollywood stars, politicians or someone you work who thinks just a bit higher of themselves than everyone else does. Healthy self-esteem is good and often times counseling is building self-esteem because it has been knocked down by something or someone but it is important to be realistic and know that our self-worth is from God. When we start evaluating ourselves compared to the world's standards (how much we have, our title, where we live, what we drive, the clothes we wear) then we are setting ourselves up to be disappointed. There will always be someone who has "more" that we think should be ours. But if we evaluate ourselves against the teachings Jesus gave us then our outlook is much different.

Let's start by taking a look at how you view others. Are you consciously aware of others feelings or how your words/actions can impact someone? Do you think that you are better than some people and therefore they do not deserve your time, attention, thoughts or prayers? Do you pray for others or usually just yourself and immediate family? Do you make promises to people that you have no intention of keeping?

Counseling teenagers can be a great deal of fun; frustrating but much fun. For a while, much of my practice was working with teenagers that were in the custody of family services, referred by the court system or having a great deal of trouble in school. For kids that are in foster care let me say that foster parents are some of the greatest saints there are because these kids often come with emotional baggage that the foster parents get to experience. One of the common personality traits of the teenagers in the system is strong self-esteem. It's a defense mechanism because often they are so insecure they are screaming, crying, hurting inside but they don't dare let that show. One of the ways of getting kids and more often adults with high self-esteem to check reality is to ask them how they want others to think of them. The common response is "I don't care what others think," or "they know I'm the greatest" but when we start talking about their response, often they realize that it's unrealistic and not going to last.

But this can go well beyond being a teenager. What about your spouse who never shows a humble side: how does that impact how you feel? At work, do you feel entitled because of how great an employee you are and therefore the company should go above and beyond for you? Let's look at a few more passages regarding humility:

2 Chronicles 7:14 Then if my people who are called by my name will humble themselves and pray and seek my face and turn from their wicked ways, I will hear from heaven and will forgive their sins and restore their land.

Psalm 25:9 He leads the humble in doing right, teaching them his way.

Proverbs 3:34 The LORD mocks the mockers but is gracious to the humble.

Matt 11:28-29 Then Jesus said, "Come to me, all of you who are weary and carry heavy burdens, and I will give you rest. Take my yoke upon you. Let me teach you, because I am humble and gentle at heart, and you will find rest for your souls.

James 4:10 Humble yourselves before the Lord, and he will lift you up in honor.

Proverbs 11:2 Pride leads to disgrace, but with humility comes wisdom.

Matt 23: 11-12 the greatest among you must be a servant. But those who exalt themselves will be humbled, and those who humble themselves will be exalted.

In these verses, look at what humility provides: sin forgiven and land healed, education, grace, rest, lifted up, wisdom, exalted. Isn't it interesting that if you first humble yourself, God will exalt you? I would much rather have these gifts than the temporary feeling when I choose to exalt myself.

The lack of humility can be very devastating to all your relationships. I've witnessed many marriages end because of selfishness. Angry and hurt children due to their parents exalting of themselves with work or hobbies. Relationships at work have ended or caused such disruption that productivity and morale are greatly impacted and focus is now a human resource issue instead of focus on the job. Church is not immune from the impact of selfish individuals or groups. Think to your own church and what would it be like if all members thought of other's needs?

The most damaging relationship is with God. We just looked at several passages on what God says about humility. How do you feel when you put everything else before Him? I know when that happens to me, I feel distant, lose focus, and start thinking much more about what I need to do instead of resting in God's presence. Remember, God never leaves us; His spirit is always with us. When we feel a disconnect in the relationship, it's because we have moved.

How do you overcome selfishness and become humble? It all starts with God. Go back and reread the passages, meditate on what they say. Take a look at all the areas of your life and where you need to show humility. Then get on your knees and pray. Let God's spirit start to transform you.

Personal application

Steve and Ruth are some of the most humble individuals I know yet they have done so much for their family, church and community. I wanted to know what God's word, the teachings of Jesus or watching someone else taught them about humility and how has that impacted their dealing with others?

- God tells us over and over in His word that we cannot approach Him without Humility.
- We need to recognize Who He is and that we are His creation that He loves and cares about.
- I love reading the Psalms and see how many times the different writers talk about what God has done: creation and all its glory, bringing out the Israelites using miracles, and His fighting on their behalf over and over through the centuries. They are constantly reminding people just Who God is by what He has done.
- When I look at WHO God is, it is very humbling to think that He knows everything about me and yet still created me.
- Psalm 139 is a very humbling psalm. I am reminded that God created every one of us and has a plan for each of our lives. We are not accidents.
- I love the passage in 1 Chronicles where King David enters the tabernacle after it has been brought into Jerusalem and sits before the Lord to tell God, "Who am I that you would bless me like you have?" That is the way I feel so much of the time.
- When I read the gospels, I see how Jesus responded and treated people everywhere He went. He never turned them away but loved them and answered their questions, healed their illnesses, taught them about God's love and how valuable they were to Him.
- Jesus showed by His example that people, even those who wanted to kill Him and gave Him a hard time, were important to God. It is a reminder to see people the way He did and not judge them by their actions or words.
- God sees all of us the same: people who are lost and hurting and need Him controlling their lives.

LOVE

1 Corinthians 13:4-8a, 13 Love is patient, love is kind. It does not envy, it does not boast, it is not proud. It is not rude, it is not self-seeking, it is not easily angered, it keeps no record of wrongs. Love does not delight in evil but rejoices with the truth. It always protects, always trusts, always hopes, always perseveres. Love never fails. And now these three remain: faith, hope and love. But the greatest of these is love.

1 Corinthians 13 is by far one of my favorite chapters in the bible. It's only thirteen verses but says so much about relationships and how we should treat each other. The verses above tell you everything you need to have a happy marriage, parent your kids, treat your parents, respect co-workers and live amongst your neighbors.

Let's take a look at how important love is. If I can speak all the languages of men or angels, or have the gift of prophecy and all knowledge, or faith that moves mountains, or give all I possess to the poor but I do not love, I have nothing. Even when measured against faith and hope, love wins. Love seems pretty important and we've been told how to love but why is it so hard to do?

We all love but the question comes down to what we love. Are you consumed by the world where what you love are possessions? Are you focused on getting the newest, fastest sports car or moving up the corporate ladder regardless of who is in your way? Maybe you are married or in a relationship but you are so consumed with winning that you must win every argument whether you are right or wrong (hint: most of the time you will be wrong). Have you become so full of pride that you ignore others needs to the point where you sometimes do not acknowledge others exist because you believe they are beneath you?

What about giving into temptation due to selfishness and indulged because the world said you could even though you knew it was wrong?

As you might have guessed, God's view of love is not the world's view. God has a specific plan for you that includes love in all areas. Let's look at a few verses where God tells what love does:

> *Psalm 23:1-6 The Lord is my shepherd, I shall not be in want. He makes me lie down in green pastures, he leads me beside quiet waters, he restores my soul. He guides me in paths of righteousness for his name's sake. Even though I walk through the valley of the shadow of death, I will fear no evil, for you are with me; your rod and your staff, they comfort me. You prepare a table before me in the presence of my enemies. You anoint my head with oil; my cup overflows. Surely goodness and love will follow me all the days of my life, and I will dwell in the house of the Lord forever.*

Love calms, is righteous, overcomes fears, provides comfort, follows us all our days.
Psalm 25:4-7 Show me your ways, O Lord, teach me your paths; guide me in your truth and teach me, for you are God my Savior, and my hope is in you all day long. Remember, O Lord, your great mercy and love, for they are from of old. Remember not the sins of my youth and my rebellious ways; according to your love remember me, for you are good, O Lord.
Love teaches, guides, provides hope and remembers good.

> *Psalm 31:13-16 For I hear the slander of many; there is terror on every side; they conspire against me and plot to take my life. But I trust in you, O Lord; I say, "You are my God." My times are in your hands; deliver me from my enemies and from those who pursue me. Let your face shine on your servant; save me in your unfailing love.*

Love saves, love trusts, love protects from evil.

> *Psalm 32:10 Many are the woes of the wicked, but the Lord's unfailing love surrounds the man who trusts in him.*

Love trusts and overcomes evil.

Psalm 36:5-7 Your love, O Lord, reaches to the heavens, your faithfulness to the skies. Your righteousness is like the mighty mountains, your justice like the great deep. O Lord, you preserve both man and beast. How priceless is your unfailing love! Both high and low among men find refuge in the shadow of your wings.

Love is faithful, preserves and is priceless. Love knows no boundaries.

Psalm 63:1-5 O God, you are my God, earnestly I seek you; my soul thirsts for you, my body longs for you, in a dry and wary land where there is no water. I have seen you in the sanctuary and beheld your power and your glory. Because your love is better than life, my lips will glorify you. I will praise you as long as I live, and in your name I will lift up my hands. My soul will be satisfied as with the richest of foods; with singing lips my mouth will praise you.

Love seeks, thirsts, glorifies, praises, satisfies.

Psalm 66:20 Praise be to God, who has not rejected my prayer or withheld his love from me!

Love does not reject or is withheld.

Romans 5:5-8 And hope does not disappoint us, because God has poured out his love into our hearts by the Holy Spirit, whom he has given us. You see, at just the right time, when we were still powerless, Christ died for the ungodly. Very rarely will anyone die for a righteous man, though for a good man someone might possibly dare to die. But God demonstrates his own love for us in this: While we were still sinners, Christ died for us.

Love reconciles and is sacrificial. Loves timing is perfect.

Romans 8:28-39 And we know that in all things God works for the good of those who love him, who have been called according to his purpose. For those God foreknew he also predestined to be conformed to the likeness of his Son, that he might be the firstborn among many brothers. And those he predestined, he also called; those he called, he also justified; those he justified, he also glorified. What, then, shall we say in response to this? If God is for us, who can be against us? He who did not spare his own Son, but gave him up for us all—how will he not also, along with him, graciously give us all things? Who will bring any charge against those who God has chosen? It is God who justifies, Who is he that condemns? Christ Jesus, who died more than that, who was raised to life—is at the right hand of God and is also interceding for us. Who shall separate us from the love of Christ? Shall trouble or hardship or persecution or famine or nakedness or danger or sword? As it is written: "For your sake we face death all day long; we are considered as sheep to be slaughtered." No, in all these things we are more than conquerors through him who loved us. For I am convinced that neither death nor life, neither angels nor demons, neither the present nor the future, nor any powers, neither height nor depth, nor anything else in all creation, will be able to separate us from the love of God that is in Christ Jesus our Lord.

Love has purpose, justifies, glorifies. Love never separates.

Romans 12:9-21 Love must be sincere. Hate what is evil; cling to what is good. Be devoted to one another in brotherly love. Honor one another above yourselves. Never be lacking in zeal, but keep your spiritual fervor, serving the Lord. Be joyful in hope, patient in affliction, faithful in prayer. Share with God's people who are in need. Practice hospitality. Bless those who persecute you; bless and do not curse. Rejoice with those who rejoice; mourn with those who mourn. Live in harmony with one another. Do not be proud, but be willing to associate with people of low position. Do not be conceited. Do not repay anyone evil for evil. Be careful to do what is right in the eyes of everybody. If it is possible, as far as it depends on you, live at peace with everyone. Do not take revenge, my friends, but leave room for God's wrath, for it is written: "It is mine to avenge; I will repay," says the Lord. On the contrary: "If your enemy is hungry, feed him; if he is thirsty, give him something to drink. In doing this, you will heap burning coals on his head.: Do not be overcome by evil, but overcome evil with good.

Love is sincere, clings to good, is devoted, honors one another, is joyful and rejoices.

1 Corinthians 13:4-8 Love is patient, love is kind. It does not envy, it does not boast, it is not proud. It is not rude, it is not self-seeking, it is not easily angered, it keeps no record of wrongs. Love does not delight in evil but rejoices with the truth. It always protects, always trusts, always hopes, always perseveres. Love never fails.

Love is patient, kind, does not envy or boast and is not proud. It is not rude or easily angered. Love always protects, always trusts, always hopes, always perseveres and never, ever fails.

This is just a sampling of what God has to say about love but the point is made that it is an important topic. In fact, my bible has 326 references to love. Without love, nothing else matters.

Jesus was the perfect example of love. He taught us how to live. He was patient with the disciples. He was faithful and most definitely sacrificial. And, when he voluntarily went to the cross, although he was the only one to never commit a sin, he paid the price for our sins that we deserve. You want an example of how to love, look at Jesus.

So, here's a few things for you to ponder and do some self reflection. The goal of these questions is to get you focused and really think about **how** you love. Best way to do this exercise is to write out your response so write in the book on get pen/paper. If you are reading electronically you get a pass but at some point put your answers in written form so you can look at your responses.

1) **What** are the material possessions you love?
2) **Who** are the people you love?
3) **Name** the things that you are really passionate about?
4) Review the list of what love does from the previous verses. Name five ways that you show love.
5) Review the list again from the above verses. What five ways do you like to be shown love?

Now that you have your list, lets compare them.

- Being honest, do you feel more passionate about your possessions, the people in your life or something else?
- Taking a look at the five ways you show love, would those individuals you love respond the same way, with the same answers?
- Regarding the ways that you like to have love shown to you, do you have people in your life that provide you with this type of love?

Let's do another quick exercise that you should write on paper as well:

- List the names of people you do not love.

I'm not talking about people you do not know but this is more about people who you would say annoy you, dislike or perhaps even hate. Is this an easy list to come up that just roll off the tongue? Is it a longer list than the list of people you love? If so, might I suggest that you are out of balance and my clinical impression would be that you are generally not happy and do not see much good in people.

If you are loved, give love and understand the sacrifices that Jesus made for you. I encourage you to continue to be an example in the world, share your love with others and continue to grow your relationship with God. However, if you have been reading this chapter and some of the verses really spoke to you or the questions pointed out some changes you want to make then I have a few suggestions.

- Reflect back to times where there was opportunity for love but did not happen. This could be in your childhood or as a young adult but think about those early relationships to see if there was an issue.
- Daily, think about ways that you can make a difference. Hold the door open for someone; tell your co-worker they did a good job on a project; buy your wife flowers just because; take the kids out for ice cream just because its Tuesday night; send a friend fudge because you know its her favorite.
- Read God's word: remember, there are 326 reference to love, read them, study the passages and then…..
- PRAY – you should always be in prayer but be specific. If there are hurts/pain in your life, ask God to heal those. If you are seeking love, pray that God would bring that right person into your life. If love has let you down in the past remember that God's love never fails and He will never leave you.

Finally, you may have tried these suggestions but the hurt is too deep or feels overwhelming. Christian counseling could be helpful to you in order to address the hurt but also gently guide you through God's word in order to help with healing.

As we close this chapter, let me reiterate how important love is. God clearly tells us that without love we have nothing. Love is the basis for everything and should be what drives your thoughts and actions. Love is the message that Jesus brought us and we are given several opportunities everyday to live out this principle. Look for those changes today to show someone love and see what a difference it makes in their life and yours.

Personal application

When looking at love, a question was posed "How has God's love for you impacted the way you love others?" While we love people different ways, i.e. love for your spouse looks different than the love for a friend or child, there are some characteristics that apply to all:

- Integrity, trust and partnership (and a sense of humor!) should always be included in love.

- When you have a loving relationship with God, loving others becomes ingrained. It is just something that you do and you pray for the ability to see others the way God sees them.
- Sometimes the best way to tell someone about God's love is to show them love through your actions and words to them.
- Love can be very frustrating but you want others to long for God and develop that same type of relationship so you stay persistent and love.
- Loving the "hard to love" is where true love shines.
- Never give up on someone, you never know when or what difference it will make.

PARENTING

Psalm 78: 1-8 O my people, hear my teaching; listen to the words of my mouth. I will open my mouth in parables, I will utter hidden things, things from of old—what we have heard and known, what our fathers have told us. We will not hide them from their children; we will tell the next generation the praiseworthy deeds of the Lord, his power, and the wonders he has done. He decreed statutes for Jacob and established the law in Israel, which he commanded our forefathers to teach their children, so the next generation would know them, even the children yet to be born, and they in turn would tell their children. Then they would put their trust in God and would not forget his deeds but would keep his commands. They would not be like their forefathers—a stubborn and rebellious generation, whose hearts were not loyal to God, whose spirits were not faithful to him.

Parenting is one of the most wonderful, joyous, exciting, rewarding, frustrating, trying, tests of patience that you will ever experience. As a dad to three of the greatest kids ever I can say, beyond a doubt that they are the greatest blessings I have been given. In no way do I deserve the fantastic, loving children we have and I hope that all parents feel the same way, even during the testing, trying and troubled times.

Notice, I did not mention they are perfect because only Christ can claim that distinction. Children are a blessing to the world from God and we all have a responsibility to help them in their walk to faith. Whether you have children or not, you play a role: you may teach, protect, heal and pray for children whether your own or others. Children need the guidance, protection and love of adults and those are roles we can all play.

This chapter is not designed to provide specific advice on how to address challenging children. There are many resources that you can further explore for specific needs in the recommended readings. For this chapter, I want to spend time talking about how you can prepare your home to help your children grow their relationship with God. Dr. Michelle Anthony has written a book titled "Spiritual Parenting" which identifies some of these concepts. Based on Dr. Anthony's environments and my own experiences as a counselor and dad, I wanted to discuss some of the ideas that I feel are most important to spiritual parenting.

Storytelling

You might think that you are a very good storyteller and can tell bedtime stories with the best of them. However, I want to talk about two different kinds of storytelling.

The first is being able to tell God's story, the story of the bible. Do you feel confident in your ability to tell God's story from Genesis to Revelation? Can you explain the fall? How about the prophets, judges, kings? Can you tell how the Old Testament and New Testament are connected? How do you explain who Jesus was and is to come? How do you even begin to tell the story of Revelation?

Being able to tell God's story is important for many reasons. First, you need to know what the bible says for your own spiritual growth. Second, you need to be able to share with your children. If your children attend Sunday school or other church groups, they should be reviewing the bible and have questions for you that you can enhance what they already learned. Some of the greatest teachable moments happen when you sit down with your child and the bible. Third, in order to witness to others, you need to know the story. Without the knowledge of the bible you will not be as effective witness as you could be.

The second kind of storytelling involves your ability to tell your personal story of salvation. At some point, your personal story will be told to your children. They will want to hear about your walk, struggles, growth, battles and trust you have in the Lord. Your story will make their walk real and show them the path. Your ability to share your story will also be important as a witness. When a nonbeliever asks about your relationship with God, will you be able to share with them in a way that moves them closer to God or do you tell the story without passion and excitement? See, anytime you tell your story of how God saved you, how He continues to guide you, the gratitude you have for the debt Jesus paid for you, there should be excitement that can hardly be contained. There should never be a boring salvation story told!

Identity

1 Peter 5:8 reminds us who wants to influence us: the devil.

> *Be self-controlled and alert. Your enemy the devil prowls around like a roaring lion looking for someone to devour.*

I believe that we often do not take Satan seriously. Satan is constantly looking to see how he can influence you, your children, all of us. We are constantly bombarded with temptation and influences that move us away from closeness with God. Our identity and the identity we grow in our children needs to be focused on God's word and desire.

What should your identity be and the identity of your child: love, joy, peace, patience, kindness, goodness, faithfulness, gentleness and self-control; the fruits of the Spirit found in Galatians 5:22-23. It is important that you as a parent spend time cultivating these fruits in your child. Know which their strengths are; which one's do they need to model you? Where are there opportunities to test and grow each of these fruits?

It is vital that you work on establishing your child's identity before outside forces get hold. In my experience, your years of being the primary influence are becoming fewer. On average, the world (friends, music, movies, school, etc) will begin to have more of an influence than you by the preteen years and with the continued rapid advances in technology your time of influence will continue to dwindle. You do not have very long to try and establish a good, solid identity foundation in your child.

Service

Just a few words about service. We are all called to serve and to do so with an attitude of love, joy and humility.

> *Philippians 2:1-4 If you have any encouragement from being united with Christ, if any comfort from his love, if any fellowship with the Spirit, if any tenderness and compassion, then make my joy complete by being*

like-minded, having the same love, being one in spirit and purpose. Do nothing out of selfish ambition or vain conceit, but in humility consider others better than yourselves. Each of you should look not only to your own interests, but also to the interests of others.

That being said, there are always opportunities to serve. Look around your own church, neighborhood for places to serve as everywhere is the mission field.

Being from the Midwest we are prone to severe storms. Some of the best service opportunities come following a tragedy when people come together to support each other in time of need. However, it does not always have to be a tragedy or time of need to serve. Look for opportunities and include your children at an early age. If you develop the spirit in them early it will carry on as an adult.

Responsibility

As you look around today there are way too many people who do not take personal responsibility. People love to blame others, or the weather, or bad luck or God when they make a mistake. However, when we are responsible, we are accountable. We begin to look at others needs and take responsibility for our family and others who need. The book of Acts focuses on those who gave out of a sense of responsibility. If someone needed time, talents, money, meals, the church gave. They lived what they believed and walked the walk.

> *Acts 4:32-35 All the believers wee one in heart and mind. No one claimed that any of his possessions was his own, but they shared everything they had. With great power the apostles continued to testify to the resurrection of he Lord Jesus, and much grace was upon them all. There were no needy persons among them. For from time to time those who owned lands or houses sold them, brought the money from the sales and put it at the apostles' feet, and it was distributed to anyone as he had need.*

As parents, we have the responsibility to make sure we raise children who will be responsible adults. Luke 2:52 shows us four areas that are important growth areas for a child:

And Jesus grew in wisdom and stature, and in favor with God and men.

Wisdom – intellectual/mental growth
Stature – physical growth
Favor with God – spiritual growth
Favor with men – social growth

As parents, we have the responsibility to teach our children, grow them intellectually and challenge them mentally. We are responsible for their physical growth, to feed them, protect and provide for them so they grow strong and healthy. We focus on their opportunity to know and walk with God, to grow spiritually by learning of His word. Finally, we create opportunities for social growth through school, church, sports, music and other activities where social rules and companionship can grow.

Course correction

Course correction, or discipline, is sometimes a challenge. We have some parents who only discipline and never show love. Other parents want to be their child's best friend and therefore never correct behavior. Hebrews 12: 1-13 focuses on why discipline is important and how God views a course correction.

Hebrews 12:1-13 Therefore, since we are surrounded by such a great cloud of witnesses, let us throw off everything that hinders and the sin that so easily entangles. And let us run with perseverance the race marked out for us, fixing our eyes on Jesus, the pioneer and perfecter of faith. For the joy set before him he endured the cross, scorning its shame, and sat down at the right hand of the throne of God. Consider him who endured such opposition from sinners, so that you will not grow weary and lose heart. In your struggle against sin, you have not yet resisted to the point of shedding your blood. And have you completely forgotten this word of encouragement that addresses you as a father addresses his son? It says, "My son, do not make light of the Lord's discipline, and do not lose heart when he rebukes you, because the Lord disciplines the one he loves, and he chastens everyone he accepts as his son." Endure hardship as discipline; God is treating you as his children. For what children are not disciplined by their father? If you are not disciplined—and everyone undergoes discipline—then you are not legitimate, not true sons and daughters at all. Moreover, we have all had human fathers who disciplined us and we respected them for it. How much more should we submit to the Father of spirits and live! They disciplined us for a little while as they thought best; but God disciplines us for our good, in order that we may share in his holiness. No discipline seems pleasant at the time, but painful. Later on, however, it produces a harvest of righteousness and peace for those who have been trained by it. Therefore, strengthen your feeble arms and weak knees. "Make level paths for your feet," so that the lame may not be disabled, but rather healed.

God disciplines those He loves: His children. He does this for our good that we may share in His holiness. It is not pleasant at the time but instead painful. However, the discipline produces righteousness and peace for those who have been trained.

As God often does, He has laid out what discipline should look like. There is a three step process:

1) Pain—This is not just physical pain and is different for everyone. Some younger children it is spankings, others it is a timeout or grounding but think back to your discipline; your course changed when there was some type of pain that you felt.
2) Build your child up in love—Reassure them, encourage, offer affection even if they do not feel like being affectionate. Speak **to** your child and not **at** your child. A reminder: which ever parent that provides the pain part of the discipline needs to bring the love piece.
3) Make a straight and level path—Show them the path you want them to take. Show your child how to change and pray that God will help them make the change.

Discipline is extremely hard and you may find yourself correcting for the same thing several times. Stay consistent and focused. Be patient. The work that you do now will pay off as you see behaviors change and your relationships grow even stronger.

Love and Respect

We spoke about love in a previous chapter but this love is specific for your children. Love for your children must be unconditional because often, especially at younger ages, you will not receive the same type of love back. Think of the sacrifices you provide for a newborn: you change diapers, feed, change diapers and feed. You are showing great love knowing that you will not be receiving the same type back. What you do get is that precious smile and cute giggle eventually that makes it all worth the sacrifice that you showed. Love and respect when raising teenagers is always a struggle as they fight for independence and you fight to hold tight. However, with love you will gradually loosen the reigns and they will gladly take them, hopefully.

Love and respect when parenting build four primary needs for your child: trust, confidence, safety and security. All four are vital in your child's development. They need to have these four needs met by someone. It can be you or they will search for someone else eventually who will provide some semblance of love. Without these needs being established children are subjected to feel guilt, shame, confusion and fear.

It is also important that you know the parenting style for which you were raised because it influences how you parent. They are mentioned briefly here:

1) Raised with authentic love – unconditional, sacrificing, active parents
2) Told you were loved but neglected – causes great confusion
3) You had to be the caregiver because your parents could not or would not
4) You were provided for but authentic love was not provided – had everything materially but never told you were loved

Know the style you were raised and correct your parenting style if needed. You can be the generation that changes and breaks the cycle. If your parents provided your authentic love, might I suggest you call them or write a nice letter thanking them for how they raised you and the impact it has on your own parenting style.

A word about respect because some parents struggle thinking respect is a one way street. When we talk about respecting your child, its more about doing the following when communicating:

- Listen generously with good focus to what they are saying
- Make good eye contact with them
- Physically be at their level, not a towering position of authority
- Have a conversation <u>with</u> them not <u>at</u> them
- Model respect first so they know how to return respect to you

Remember 1 Corinthians 13, love is patient, kind, it does not envy, it does boast, it is not proud. It is not rude, it is not self-seeking, it is not easily angered, it keeps no record of wrongs. Love does not delight in evil but rejoices with the truth. It always protects, always trusts, always hopes, always perseveres. Love never fails.

Unconditional love can be very frustrating but it is well worth the time and commitment that you make for your child. With love and respect they will grow to be mature, caring adults. Without, they will spend a lifetime seeking to fill a void.

Modeling

This might be the most important concept. It is amazing how observant children are. They spend their entire lifetime watching you to see how you are going to react, respond, threat others. Their initial ideas on how to be a friend, spouse, employee and parent will all come from watching you. I know that is a lot of pressure but that is the reality.

> *Ephesians 5: 1-5 Be imitators of God, therefore, as dearly loved children and live a life of love, just as Christ loved us and gave himself up for us as a fragrant offering and sacrifice to God. But among you there must not be even a hint of sexual immorality, or of any kind of impurity, or of greed, because these are improper for God's holy people. Nor should there be obscenity, foolish talk or coarse joking, which are out of place, but rather thanksgiving. For of this you can be sure: no immorality, impure or greedy person—such a man is an idolater—has any inheritance in the kingdom of Christ and of God.*

We should imitate God, model ourselves after the love He has shown us. If we model God's word in our life, our children will see this and hopefully want to model as well.

How do we model effectively? We are <u>honest</u> in our dealings and actions. We are <u>humble</u>, putting others first and looking to serve where needed. We <u>correct</u> our behavior when it is not consistent with God's word. We take <u>responsibility</u> for our actions and <u>ask forgiveness</u> when we have wronged someone – especially your spouse or child.

It is important to persevere and see parenting all the way through to the end. Do not become complacent; don't quit parenting because the kids hit a certain age; don't be distracted by work or hobbies or finances. Stay focused for you are building the most important relationship your child will ever have: their relationship with God.

One final question for you to ponder regarding parenting: What will your response be when you stand before God and He asks you to give an account of how you parented the children He gave you?

Personal application

Steve and Ruth have raised three children who all have personal relationships with God. However, they realize that their role in raising these blessings from God was to provide, protect and create an environment where their children could have God reveal Himself to them. As Steve and Ruth now have the joy of grandchildren they pray for God to reveal Himself to them as they grow and mature. They do have many lessons that have been learned along the way and here are some of those for us to remember and learn:

- Kids were never allowed to be disrespectful to a parent or authority figure without repercussions.
- Parenting is an opportunity to model how to treat the opposite sex. To treat each other with respect, dignity and showing love are great ways to have your kids see how a parent/spouse should treat each other.
- It's alright to let them see you disagree but always reassure them this is normal because two people won't always see things the same way. And when they ask, let them know disagreements do not result in divorce.
- It's okay to let your kids fail; remember that they are just kids, that is how they learn and grow.

- Set boundaries for your children when it comes to the friends they choose. Your job as a parent is to teach them the type of characteristics a friend should be and if someone they chose is not good for them, they need to know why.
- Give God time to develop your child's spirit and heart. Don't try to rush the work He is doing in their life.
- Discipline is unique to the personality of the child; to one, sending them to their room is punishment, to another, a stern word, and to another, a ruler to the seat of the pants.
- As your child grows and matures, the way you treat them needs to adapt. As they earn the trust, provide them with additional responsibilities and as they move into adulthood, treat them as adults.
- Have your priorities in line. If attending church is important to you then it should come before sporting events. Example of no games before noon on Sunday.
- When your kids are younger, bedtime can be very special. Use that opportunity to read bible stories to them and always pray with them each night.
- Pick your battles but do not sacrifice your values and beliefs.
- Create a memory box for your children/grandchildren that include items and letters of how you have been praying for them and encourage them as they grow to know God. The memory box can be shared on the day saved or baptized.
- As a grandparent, respect your children as they now parent. Enforce the rules <u>they</u> have set but use opportunities to still be a model or resource for your children who now are parenting.
- Always hug and tell your kids and grandkids how much you love them.
- Ask God for wisdom in parenting and to see the plan that God has for their life.
- As a task assigned by a former pastor, we once developed a family mission statement; "We will have reverence for God, responsibility for yourself and respect for others" (they probably don't remember it now though).
- Be nice to your children, they will be choosing your nursing home!

PATIENTLY WAITING

Romans 8:19a The creation waits in eager expectation for ….

I travel quite a bit and there is nothing like the anticipation of going home after a trip. Can't wait to get to the airport, get through security, board the plane and get home. All steps are done with eager anticipation for returning home. What happens when my return does not work out the way I had planned? Plane is delayed, then delayed again, then delayed one more time before finally canceled and the nice airline person tells you "sorry, first flight out is tomorrow."

We wait in eager expectation for (fill in the blank). Kids wait for school to be done. We wait eagerly to get married or have kids. We eagerly wait for a new job or promotion. We eagerly wait for our paycheck or our favorite meal. But do we wait in eager expectation for God?

There are examples throughout the Bible that God has provided that speaks as to why waiting is important:

Psalm 40:1 I waited patiently for the Lord; he turned to me and heard my cry.

David speaks of how he patiently waited for the Lord. God heard David's cry and lifted him out of his pit and placed him on firm rock to stand.

Isaiah 30:18 Yet the Lord longs to be gracious to you; he rises to show you compassion. For the Lord is a God of justice. Blessed are all who wait for him!

Reminds us how God longs to bless those who are patient and wait for Him.

In Acts 1:4-5 On one occasion, while he was eating with them, he (Jesus) gave them this command: "Do not leave Jerusalem, but wait for the gift my Father promised, which you have heard me speak about. For John baptized with water, but in a few days you will be baptized with the Holy Spirit."

Jesus instructs us to wait for the gift God has promised, the gift of the Holy Spirit.

Romans 8:23-25 Not only so, but we ourselves, who have the firstfruits of the Spirit, groan inwardly as we wait eagerly for our adoption as sons, the redemption of our bodies. For in this hope we were saved. But hope that is seen is no hope at all. Who hopes for what he already has? But if we hope for what we do not yet have, we wait for it patiently.

We are to wait eagerly for hope, the hope that has saved us and allowed us to be adopted in God's family.

Titus 2:11-14 For the grace of God that brings salvation has appeared to all men. It teaches us to say "No" to ungodliness and worldly passions, and to live self-controlled, upright and godly lives in this present age, while we wait for the blessed hope—the glorious appearing of our great God and Savior, Jesus Christ, who gave himself for us to redeem us from all wickedness and to purify for himself a people that are his very own, eager to do what is good.

Teaches us that we wait patiently for the glorious return of Jesus.

We also learn in many other verses that patience comes from wisdom (Proverbs 19:11); can calm a quarrel (Proverbs 15:18) and goes hand in hand with joy, peace, kindness, goodness, endurance, humility and gentleness.

What God tells us through His work is that there are many benefits and blessings to being patient and waiting eagerly. Where we start to get into trouble is when we think that we have waited long enough and push the issue.

We do this all the time when we buy something we cannot afford. Or, we engage in premarital sex. Or, we marry someone we do not fully love because we do not think that there will be anyone else. We live in a time when immediate satisfaction is expected, even demanded. We want that from our 24 hour news sources, movies on demand, call centers and websites available when we want and many times we want an immediate response from God.

Only, that is not how God operates. Even the times when judgment came, God was patient and sent prophets and messages warning of outcomes. God has been our primary example of how to wait with eager expectation because He knows all the good He has planned for us.

Patiently waiting has great rewards for us. One of the best ways for us to cope with our anxiety over waiting is prayer. Prayer is our direct line to God and He understands the struggles we have with waiting. If you ask for help God will provide and you will start to see all the benefits and gifts that come from waiting with eager expectation. You will become so close to God through prayer and studying His word that waiting patiently will become a strength for you.

> *Philippians 4:4-7 Rejoice in the Lord always. I will say it again: Rejoice! Let your gentleness be evident to all. The Lord is near. Do not be anxious about anything, but in everything, by prayer and petition, with thanksgiving, present your requests to God. And the peace of God, which transcends all understanding, will guard your hearts and your minds in Christ Jesus.*

Paul, in his letter to Philippi, is telling us to rejoice even while waiting and especially when we are faced with trouble. There is never a time when we should be anxious because of our ability and relationship with God. This is an amazing gift we have been provided but how often do we let our emotions, especially anxiety and despair, get the best of us when God is saying "come to me and tell your fears, needs and requests."

One of the most difficult times to be patient is waiting for justice or seeing individuals succeed who you think should not. You don't want to see the guilty get away and want them to pay for the evil they have done. You look at people who have millions of dollars and seem set for life but you know that they have cheated, lied or scammed their way to their fortune while you work hard, try to right by God and yet you and your family struggle. You question God as to why there is one trial after another and yet you know people who mock God and never go through a tough challenge. You go through many different emotions: anger, resentment, hopelessness, helplessness, wanting to give up and frustrated.

Psalm 37 gives us words of encouragement during these very times. In this wonderful Psalm of David's, we read how God feels about the wicked and the evil they have done. Look at some of the things that will happen to the wicked:

- They will soon wither away
- They will soon die
- Evil men will be cut off
- Wicked will be no more after a little while, you will not find them
- God laughs at the wicked for He knows their day is coming
- Their swords will pierce their own heart
- Power of the wicked will be broken
- Wicked will perish
- Wicked lie in wait for the righteous, be the Lord will not leave them in power
- Ruthless men will pass away and be no more

Conversely, God shares through David what those who trust in the Lord can experience. As you might imagine it is quite a bit different than what the wicked will be experiencing:

- Instructed to not fret or be envious of those who do wrong
- Trust in the Lord and do good
- Dwell in the land and enjoy safe pasture
- Delight yourself in the Lord and receive the desires of your heart
- Commit your way to the Lord
- Refrain from anger and turn from wrath
- The meek will inherit the land and enjoy great peace
- Our inheritance will endure forever
- May stumble, but will not fall as the Lord holds you in His hand
- Lord will not forsake His faithful ones

- Will be protected forever
- The man of peace will have a future
- The salvation of the righteous comes from the Lord

Quite a difference experience for those who love, honor and trust God! But, I think this whole chapter is wrapped up in the first part of Psalm 37:7:

Be still before the Lord and wait patiently for him

It does not matter where you are or what you are experiencing, God is always before you, waiting for you to come to Him with your troubles, pain and requests. But, we are called to be patient, still and wait for God's perfect timing to answer prayers and respond to our needs. The evil and wicked may appear to be prospering now but knowing what's coming their way, I would not want to trade places with them for all the gold in the world.

Personal Application

Steve and Ruth have done experienced a long and fruitful life which means plenty of opportunity for waiting patiently. I wanted to know what were some of the lessons they learned while waiting for something eagerly that was happening on God's timetable and not theirs.

- The past 2 years I have especially been impressed with the fact that God's time is so very important and we need to wait on Him.
- When I look back on so many things through our lives, I can see how God worked on a person's heart or circumstances to bring them to Him.
- I think especially of a person finally understanding that God has offered them His great salvation and they accept Him and turn their lives over to Him.
- I also think about some frustrating times waiting for an answer to a problem and then God shows me a direction in a special way.

- I'm learning to be more patient and ask Him for peace while I'm waiting for Him to work. I have to remind myself that He sees the whole picture and knows what is down the road.
- If I push to get my way in my time, I will mess things up.
- He sometimes allows us to get what we ask for as a lesson to teach us He knows what is best for us.
- Patiently waiting looks much different as one becomes older. Could be maturity but the way life and waiting looks at 60 is much different than it looked at 20.
- Sometimes God uses a life changing event to impact how we wait. Often this is God using His timing to break our will and show us that He is in control. Once we surrender and give up trying to control a situation we have a sense of peace and understanding that is not present when we are trying to control. God's Will should always trump our desire for personal control.

POLITICS

1 John 3:7 Dear children, do not let anyone lead you astray. He who does what is right is righteous.

We are at the point in politics when candidates are always campaigning. Even those who have recently won an election are busy fundraising and talking about a potential next opponent. It would be interesting to see what could happen if leaders actually governed instead of constantly looking at the next election.

Faith and God always seem to play a prominent role in any political campaign. All candidates want to capture the Christian vote and will say almost anything to show that they have a strong faith and therefore deserve your vote. However, do their actions accurately reflect what they say?

There are a few "hot" political topics that always seem to be present in the most recent elections and will most likely continue because of the passion that exists on both sides. My goal is to see what the Bible says about these topics and hope that you and our leaders use these teachings in how we vote and how they lead.

<u>*Marriage:*</u>

The traditional view of one man/one woman has become a political issue over the past several election cycles. Recent debates include allowing a redefinition of marriage. Here are a few bible passages that express God's view of marriage:

> *Genesis 2:23-24 "At last!" the man exclaimed. "This one is bone from my bone, and flesh from my flesh! She will be called 'woman,' because she was*

taken from 'man.'" This explains why a man leaves his father and mother and is joined to his wife, and the two are united into one.

1 Corinthians 7:2-3 But because there is so much sexual immorality, each man should have his own wife, and each woman should have her own husband. The husband should fulfill his wife's sexual needs, and the wife should fulfill her husband's needs.

Matthew 19:4-6 "Haven't you read," he replied, "that at the beginning the Creator 'made them male and female,' and said, 'For this reason a man will leave his father and mother and be united to his wife, and the two will become one flesh'? So they are no longer two, but one. Therefore what God has joined together, let man not separate."

<u>Abortion:</u>

This has been a political/legal debate since Roe v Wade in 1973. While abortion is legal, much of the political debate at this point surrounds the Supreme Court and the influence the next appointees could have regarding a challenge. Thus, the public always wants to know candidates, especially for President, stance. The Bible has the following to say regarding the unborn:

Jeremiah 1:5 "Before I formed you in the womb I knew you, before you were born I set you apart"

Luke 1:44 "As soon as the sound of your greeting reached my ears, the baby in my womb leaped for joy."

Exodus 20:13 "You shall not murder"

Psalm 139:13-16 For you created my inmost being; you knit me together in my mother's womb. I praise you because I am fearfully and wonderfully made; your works are wonderful, I know that full well. My frame was not hidden from you when I was made in the secret place. When I was woven together in the depths of the earth, your eyes saw my unformed body. All the days ordained for me were written in your book before one of them came to be.

Taxes:

I use to think that nobody wanted to pay taxes but recently we have individuals who are advocating paying more. The ongoing debate in the current political season is redistribution of income. Taxes and the next topic, debt, often are in the same discussion read all passages with both in mind:

Romans 13:5-7 "Therefore, it is necessary to submit to the authorities, not only because of possible punishment but also because of conscience. This is also why you pay taxes, for the authorities are God's servants, who give their full time to governing. Give everyone what you owe him: If you owe taxes, pay taxes; if revenue, then revenue; if respect, then respect; if honor, then honor.

Matthew 22:15-22 "Then the Pharisees went out and laid plans to trap him in his words. They sent their disciples to him along with the Herodians. 'Teacher,' they said, 'we know you are a man of integrity and that you teach the way of God in accordance with the truth. You aren't swayed by men, because you pay no attention to who they are. Tell us then, what is your opinion? Is it right to pay taxes to Caesar or not?' But Jesus, knowing their evil intent, said, 'You hypocrites, why are you trying to trap me? Show me the coin used for paying the tax.' They brought him a denarius, and he asked them, 'Whose portrait is this? And whose inscription?' 'Caesar's,' they replied. Then he said to them, 'Give to Caesar what is Caesar's and to God what is God's.' When they heard this, they were amazed. So they left him and went away."

Luke 16:10-12 "Whoever can be trusted with very little can also be trusted with much, and whoever is dishonest with very little will also be dishonest with much. So if you have not been trustworthy in handling worldly wealth, who will trust you with true riches? And if you have not been trustworthy with someone else's property, who will give you property of your own?"

Luke 3:12-13 "Tax collectors also came to be baptized. 'Teacher,' they asked, 'what should we do?' 'Don't collect any more than you are required to,' he told them.

Debt:

The news leads most every night with the current debt crisis. European countries on the brink of bankruptcy; the US debt is well into the **_trillions_** of dollars. Personal/family debt is at all-time highs with many struggling to find any way out. There are good resources to help an individual or family start attacking their debt but what about countries? Debt is a behavior – live within your means. If you can't afford it, don't buy it…same should go for countries.

Proverbs 22:7 "The rich rule over the poor, and the borrower is servant to the lender."

Romans 13:8 "Let no debt remain outstanding, except the continuing debt to love one another, for he who loves his fellowman has fulfilled the law."

Hope:

Every election involves hope. Hope that whatever is going wrong will be changed and hope that whatever is going right will continue. The Bible is very clear on where you hope should be. Hint: your hope should not be in the government or any worldly leader.

Psalm 42:5-6a "Why are you downcast, O my soul? Why so disturbed within me? Put your hope in God, for I will yet praise him, my Savior and my God."

Psalm 62:5-6 "Find rest, O my soul, in God alone; my hope comes from him. He alone is my rock and my salvation; he is my fortress, I will not be shaken."

Psalm 119:74 "May those who fear you rejoice when they see me, for I have put my hope in your word."

Romans 5:5 "Hope does not disappoint us, because God has poured out his love into our hearts by the Holy Spirit, whom he has given us."

Romans 15:4 "For everything that was written in the past was written to teach us, so that through endurance and the encouragement of the Scriptures we might have hope."

1 Timothy 6:17 "Command those who are rich in this present world not to be arrogant nor to put their hope in wealth, which is so uncertain, but to put their hope in God, who richly provides us with everything for our enjoyment.

<u>*Poor:*</u>

There have always been poor people and no government intervention can solve this entire issue. The Bible speaks of them often but politicians speak of them all the time. One political view is to provide the poor with government aid i.e. income redistribution, government subsidies. Another side wants to provide skills training and create better job opportunities. Both sides want to help; it's just a matter on what side you fall. Notice, the verses instruct an individual responsibility to give out of the kindness of your heart. Here is the side the Bible takes:

Deuteronomy 15:10-11 "Give generously to him and do so without a grudging heart; then because of this the Lord your God will bless you in all your work and in everything you put your hand to. There will always be poor people in the land. Therefore I command you to be openhanded toward your brothers and toward the poor and needy in your land."

Proverbs 14:31 "He who oppresses the poor shows contempt for their Maker, but whoever is kind to the needy honors God."

Proverbs 19:17 "He who is kind to the poor lends to the Lord, and he will reward him for what he has done."

Proverbs 22:9 "A generous man will himself be blessed, for he shares his food with the poor."

Proverbs 31:20 "She opens her arms to the poor and extends her hands to the needy."

<u>Serving:</u>

You might be wondering why serving is included in a politics chapter. I get the sense that politicians have forgotten that they are "public servants" elected to serve. Jesus and the apostle Paul had a great deal to say about serving. Perhaps we should send these verses to our elected servants:

Matthew 20:24-28 When the ten others heard about this, they lost their tempers, thoroughly disgusted with the two brothers. So Jesus got them together to settle things down. He said, "You've observed how godless rulers throw their weight around, how quickly a little power goes to their heads. It's not going to be that way with you. Whoever wants to be great must become a servant. Whoever wants to be first among you must be your slave. That is what the Son of Man has done: He came to serve, not be served—and then to give away his life in exchange for the many who are held hostage."

Matthew 25:21 The master was full of praise. 'Well done, my good and faithful servant. You have been faithful in handling this small amount, so now I will give you many more responsibilities. Let's celebrate together!

Philippians 2:4-7 Each of you should look not only to your own interests, but also to the interests of others. Your attitude should be the same as that of Christ Jesus: Who, being in very nature with God, did not consider equality with God something to be grasped, but made himself nothing, taking the very nature of a servant, being made in human likeness.

Joshua 22:5 But be very careful to obey all the commands and the instructions that Moses gave to you. Love the LORD your God, walk in all his ways, obey his commands, hold firmly to him, and serve him with all your heart and all your soul.

Ephesians 4:11-12 Now these are the gifts Christ gave to the church: the apostles, the prophets, the evangelists, and the pastors and teachers. Their responsibility is to equip God's people to do his work and build up the church, the body of Christ.

Colossians 3:23-24 Work willingly at whatever you do, as though you were working for the Lord rather than for people. Remember that the Lord will give you an inheritance as your reward, and that the Master you are serving is Christ.

Romans 12:11 Never be lazy, but work hard and serve the Lord enthusiastically.

<u>*Sharing/Giving:*</u>

Sharing, redistribution, giving – for as many politicians as we have it's all called something different. If you have been reading so far, you know that God gave us blessings and gifts to share. As a Christian, you should want to share your gifts and talents. If you look back at the passages for the poor, hope and serving there is a common theme of individual responsibility and not relying on government. I have seen time and time again how individuals and communities step up when there is a need, especially during a crisis. God loving individuals want to give and share what has been provided not because of a government mandate but because of our love for God. We, as individuals, have a desire to give to others. Here is what the Bible shares regarding giving:

Ephesians 4:28 If you are a thief, quit stealing. Instead, use your hands for good hard work, and then give generously to others in need.

Luke 3:11 John replied, "If you have two shirts, give one to the poor. If you have food, share it with those who are hungry."

1 Timothy 6:18-19 Tell them to use their money to do good. They should be rich in good works and generous to those in need, always being ready to share with others. By doing this they will be storing up their treasure as a good foundation for the future so that they may experience true life.

Hebrews 13:16 And don't forget to do good and to share with those in need. These are the sacrifices that please God.

Matthew 25:34-46 "Then the King will say to those on his right, 'Come, you who are blessed by my Father, inherit the Kingdom prepared for you from the creation of the world. For I was hungry, and you fed me. I was thirsty, and you gave me a drink. I was a stranger, and you invited me into your home. I was naked, and you gave me clothing. I was sick, and you cared for me. I was in prison, and you visited me.' "Then these righteous ones will reply, 'Lord, when did we ever see you hungry and feed you? Or thirsty and give you something to drink? Or a stranger and show you hospitality? Or naked and give you clothing? When did we ever see you sick or in prison and visit you?' "And the King will say, 'I tell you the truth, when you did it to one of the least of these my brothers and sisters, you were doing it to me!' "Then the King will turn to those on the left and say, 'Away with you, you cursed ones, into the eternal fire prepared for the devil and his demons. For I was hungry, and you didn't feed me. I was thirsty, and you didn't give me a drink. I was a stranger, and you didn't invite me into your home. I was naked, and you didn't give me clothing. I was sick and in prison, and you didn't visit me.' "Then they will reply, 'Lord, when did we ever see you hungry or thirsty or a stranger or naked or sick or in prison, and not help you?' "And he will answer, 'I tell you the truth, when you refused to help the least of these my brothers and sisters, you were refusing to help me.' "And they will go away into eternal punishment, but the righteous will go into eternal life."

See, politics does not have to be difficult. God, through His word, has provided direction on most every political topic; all we need to do is read and follow His guidance. And that is perhaps what is most frustrating. We proclaim to follow God; to be a Christian nation. Our politicians are sworn into office with their hand on the Bible, sessions open with prayer but that seems to be where God's influence ends. If we truly are a nation that governs according to God's commands and wisdom then why don't we publicly consult His word when we have an issue or disagreement? Instead we have political fighting and little is accomplished. God and His word should be at the heart of every decision and not mentioned just when there is a national tragedy.

As you have just read, God has a lot to say on topics that are pertinent to today's culture. God is not surprised that we are struggling with any of these issues which are why He gave instructions and guidance. Will we finally listen?

Personal application

For personal application, I wanted to talk to a Christian politician. You may have a preconceived notion that the term Christian politician is an oxymoron but they do exist, just have to look hard in this political environment. The following thoughts come from a well-respected, Christian man who also is involved in local politics.

- Cannot check faith at the door when making political decisions. If you can, then need to reexamine if really a Christian and where else you "check your faith."
- Faith guides every decision and action. It is the basis for your morals and beliefs and therefore faith influences the actions we take. It becomes ingrained to our character.
- It is important that the image you show is a true reflection of your character. People that you represent want and need to be able to trust who you really are.
- Being a Christian public servant is respecting individual freedoms and acting to protect those freedoms until such actions impact "our" freedoms. Then the role of

the public servant is to legislate based on beliefs that have hopefully been guided by faith in Jesus.
- Biblically, it was always intended to be the role of the family, community or church to care for those in need, not the government. At some point in our culture, we became too self-centered and decided to outsource the care of the needy to the government. Not only have families adopted this approach but in many instances the church has moved to just providing for their own, not the community needs.
- Government's role of supporting those with needs should be to provide a safety net to help people survive until they can sustain themselves. It should not be to provide programs that are "life sustaining" essentially making one dependent on the government to live.
- Government should partner with community groups whose primary focus is to provide services to those with needs. Community groups can provide services much better than the government but the government can provide certain support that are not otherwise available (i.e. tax incentives, funds).
- In the end, all politicians vote what they believe. They may say something different to the public but what they truly believe is how they will vote.
- A quote from Milton Friedman, noted economist, regarding gauging policies: "One of the great mistakes is to judge policies and programs by their intentions rather than their results."

SUFFERING

Psalm 44:22 Yet for your sake we face death all day long; we are considered as sheep to be slaughtered.

It's one of the most asked questions of all time: Why does God allow suffering to occur, especially to those who follow Him? This could be a very short chapter if the answer is "we do not know, but we'll ask God when we get to Heaven." However, God gave us some insight as to why suffering does and must occur. This is important to look at for several reasons but at the top of the list for me is this question and, I believe, holds many people back in their faith. How many times have you heard or seen an interview with someone who states "if God allows a child to die or the terrorist attacks of 9/11 to occur, then I do not want anything to do with God."

In all my years of doing disaster response and helping people through tragedies, there are often two responses: one comes much closer to God and relies on Him for peace, comfort, understanding and strength or they become angry with God for allowing this to happen. Anger is definitely an emotional stage of dealing with a tragedy but is that anger in the right place and directed at the right person or thing?

Why do we suffer? The quick answer is because Jesus suffered and our suffering brings us closer to Jesus. However, this answer goes deeper if we look at some passages.

Mark 8:31 – Jesus suffered not only the physical pain, He suffered the emotional pain of rejection from His own people, the one's He was there to save.

Luke 24:26, 46-48 – *Jesus' suffering had to occur before His glory occurred. His suffering allowed repentance and forgiveness of sins to be preached in all the nations.*

Philippians 1:29-30 – *Paul, along with the other apostles, suffered physically, emotionally and many times gave their life on behalf of Jesus and their faith. Being a follower of Jesus does not eliminate you from suffering.*

1 Peter 4:12-19 – *If you are suffering, you are being grown by God and should consider it a blessing. This suffering is an opportunity to further commit ourselves to God and thus draw closer to Him.*

Hebrews 2:18 – *Because Jesus was human, He was tempted and understands the suffering that occurs from temptation. Therefore, He is able to help us we are tempted.*

1 Peter 2:20-23 – *Jesus is our example of how to respond to suffering. There is no retaliation, there are no threats, instead there is trusting God who provides judgment.*

Romans 8:17-18 – *We all share in sufferings so that we share in glory. This glory will be revealed in us at just the right time and until then we wait with great anticipation, especially through suffering.*

Suffering causes a wide arrange of emotions in us. When suffering we can become sad, depressed and angry especially when we believe the suffering is due to someone else's actions. We lose interest in things we use to find joy, we seclude ourselves from others and often we cry. We can become despondent, stop taking care of ourselves and others with whom we are responsible. We can feel hopeless and helpless and believe that the emotional pain will never end. We look for answers in a pill, needle or bottle. Unfortunately, many believe the only way to stop the pain is suicide.

These are the behaviors from suffering but still do not explain the why. All throughout the Bible, as we saw above and in other chapters, every character suffers. Every person suffers through trials in their life. Some are physical ailments that can become so overbearing that it impacts every area of your life. Other suffering is deep, emotional pain caused by mental illness, other's actions or your own actions but the emotions become so overwhelming that you cannot function. Suffering can and will impact every area of your life but do not underestimate spiritual suffering. When you are out of touch with God and your spirit suffers the pain is deeper than any other.

Peter Kreeft writes about God's answer to suffering. Kreeft's teachings suggest that the answer to suffering is not something, but someone: Jesus. Suffering is part of the relationship that we have with God. It's not so much the explanations about why suffering occurs as much as we want the assurance that everything is going to be okay. Jesus answers suffering with love. Love seeks to be present, intimate and as one. Jesus gave himself which is the greatest gift that could be given.

By coming into our world, Jesus entered all parts including our suffering. God's Spirit remains in us constantly. When we are at the lowest point of our lives, He is there. When we are broken, rejected by others, misunderstood, lost and alone, He is there. Every depth of darkness we sink, He is there. Even when we reject and move from Him, He does not leave us, instead longing for us to return. He is with us in every possible suffering we experience. There is no place to dark that He cannot shine light.

He has even shined light on the darkest of all: death. Think beyond the fact that He rose from the dead but that the meaning of death has been changed. All of what we see as the young dying, the grind of a long, slow death and even anticipated older death has been changed. This happened through the resurrection. As Jesus rose again, we have hope and knowing that God can and does raise again!

But what of the solution to suffering? Kreeft suggests that the solution to our suffering is our suffering. All suffering becomes part of God's work, the work of salvation. As long as we believe, as we have faith then we see suffering as a gift, challenge and an invitation to share with God and join closer to Him. This is our invitation to follow Christ to the cross. "Suffering is not the context that explains the cross; the cross is the context that explains suffering." In the end, it all comes down to true love. True love is willing to suffer and God came along side us in our suffering to bring us closer to Him.

Besides Jesus, the biblical character who suffered the most is Job. As review, Job is a great, Godly man who has been very blessed. We learn from Job 1:3 that he was the "greatest man among all the people of the East." God has this to say about Job's character and stature:

Job 1:8 There is no one on Earth like him; he is blameless and upright, a man who fears God and shuns evil.

This great man, who made burnt offerings for his children each morning, just in case they had sinned, became the object of a test. A test to see if, through excruciating suffering, he would curse God. Satan does his best by destroying his livestock, killing his children and finally inflicting great personal physical pain. Job is suffering in every imaginable way yet look at his responses:

Job 1:20-22 At this, Job got up and tore his robe and shaved his head. Then he fell to the ground in worship and said: "Naked I came from my mother's womb, and naked I will depart. The Lord gave and the Lord has taken away; may the name of the Lord be praised." In all this, Job did not sin by charging God with wrongdoing.

Job 2:9-10 His wife said to him, "Are you still holding on to your integrity? Curse God and die!" He replied, "You are talking like a foolish woman. Shall we accept good from God, and not trouble?" In all this, Job did not sin in what he said.

The first few times I studied Job, I thought how cruel his wife is for suggesting he "curse God and die." However, while not much is mentioned about her, you know that she is grieving. She is finding out this same information of all that is lost including her 10 children that she birthed and raised to be adults. We see what suffering parents look like only I suggest that Job's relationship with God is much stronger than his wife's. Job looks to the Lord and praises Him not only in the blessings but the trials. Job understands that good and trouble can both be part of life but will not dare curse God when times are

Suffering

difficult. However, Job's wife sees the situation differently but definitely from a grieving, suffering perspective. She has become hopeless and helpless seeing the only option for Job is him to curse God and die to end the suffering. But Job, in his suffering stands firm and attempts to be the spiritual leader for his wife as she suffers.

We then watch the next several chapters of Job unfold as he has a conversation with his friends. During this time, Job has many questions; questions that he does not have the answers nor his friends. But as we see in the end, through all his suffering and tormented experiences, he is pleased with God who provided no answers to his questions but instead because God came: He gave Himself.

But that in itself is maddening about suffering: the questions. Why does suffering occur, especially to Christians who are trying to live for God when it seems that non believers prosper or experience little suffering? Job was blameless and upright and now he finds himself embroiled in a test of his faith. Does he love and serve God because of their relationship or because God has given Job everything up to this point? Job, like us often, does not know the cause of the suffering, just that he is in it at that time. And yet, we ask still another question: Where is God in our suffering?

As Bill Crowder states: "The solution to suffering and the doubts it raises is not found in argument. It is found in learning to rest in God's grace and to trust in His power—even when the suffering is mysterious and overwhelming." God does not remove our suffering but instead we are made free because God suffers with us, He shares with us at the cross. We have hope of God's everlasting love because of this relationship.

There is no easy way through suffering. No magic pill or words that take away all the pain. Suffering happens to bring us closer to God, to build our relationship, to realize that He is our Comforter, Healer and Counselor. As a counselor, I can console you and give words of comfort but I can never fully understand your pain, grief or suffering. Only God can and He walks through every tear and painful moment that you experience. You are never abandoned, never alone, never left to suffer by yourself. The God of the universe, who created everything and sees every moment of your life, is with you.

Personal application

For this chapter, I wanted to know how Steve and Ruth saw God provide comfort, peace and healing during a time of intense suffering.

- I remember when my mother suffered with health problems for the last 15 years of her life. She never complained and when she was in the hospital, she would witness to the nurses and her Jewish doctor. She and my dad spent the last 9 years of their lives at the Baptist Home in Ironton. The Home would bring her up to St. Louis to MO Baptist and when she was there, some friends from church would visit her. After she passed away, I was angry with God for allowing her to suffer so much and then within a week's time, I had 2 different people tell me how much she meant to them because of her sweet attitude and love for the Lord. The Lord reminded me that He received the glory, due to her peace and joy that others saw in her wherever she went. That can only be explained by God's presence in her life.
- I also remember the time when she was staying with us for 2 weeks after she had surgery. I was working full time and would come home and care for her physical needs. One night, I just cried and told God I couldn't do that anymore. I loved my mom but I was so physically and emotionally exhausted. God brought to my mind His verse in Isaiah 40:31 where he says that if we wait on Him, He will give us strength to soar run and walk and right now I was just putting one foot in front of the other but He promised to give me the strength to do that. I had a sense of His peace and was able to sleep and go through the rest of the time she was with us without being so overwhelmed. My mom was a very special lady who loved the Lord and it showed in everything she did and said through her life.

TRUST

Philippians 4:4-7 Rejoice in the Lord always. I will say it again: Rejoice! Let your gentleness be evident to all. The Lord is near. Do not be anxious about anything, but in everything, by prayer and petition, with thanksgiving, present your requests to God. And the peace of God, which transcends all understanding, will guard your hearts and your minds in Christ Jesus.

Who do you trust and why? Many people want your trust: spouses, parents, friends, the government and salesmen. Do you blindly give your trust or does it have to be earned?

As you ponder these questions, let's think about times when someone you trusted let you down. Could be a business partner who stole from you; a parent that lied to you; a spouse who cheated. What did you feel when this trust was broken? There are many couples/individuals I've counseled where broken trust has been the theme. The common feelings are: anger, disappointment, betrayal, loss, devastation, despair, hopelessness, helplessness, shock and emptiness. There may be other emotions that you have felt but at some point I would guess that you experienced one or more of these feelings.

As we would work through these feelings time and time again the question would be "why?" Why would someone break the trust that you had given and choose to hurt you? One of the things we would find is that all their trust wrapped up in one individual. Don't get me wrong, we should trust those closest to us that they are not going to harm or betray us but remember that we are humans and as humans we sin and are far from perfect. We make choices that we think are protecting our loved ones. A common explanation I would hear for why a husband would lie to his wife is "I love you so much, I wanted to protect you." However, when the lie is revealed there are much bigger issues to address.

After trust is broken and the initial feelings are addressed, the next frequently asked question is, "will I ever be able to trust again?" The quick answer to this question is yes; you can and will trust again. However, there is a process and once you've been burned; trust does not come that easy. One of the places to start is to take a look at the lessons you learned from the betrayal. In the political world, a common thought is to never let a crisis go to waste. I believe that God never lets an opportunity to teach us something go to waste. This crisis you are going through is a great opportunity that God is using to teach you and draw you closer to Him.

Start by realizing that God is the only true opportunity for complete trust we have. Look back at our passage in Philippians. We can rejoice because God is always near – He is never going to leave us even when others do. There is no need for us to be anxious about anything because we know that God will provide and we should take our anxiety, fears and lack of trust to Him in prayer. And, when we feel lost and do not understand why certain things happen, we know that the peace of God is with us, sustains and strengthens us through our savior, Jesus.

Let's look at other lessons we have about trust. In Exodus 16, we see where a lack of trust in God caused stress for the Israelites, where their first thought was to return to Egypt.

Exodus 16:2-3 In the desert the whole community grumbled against Moses and Aaron. The Israelites said to them, "If only we had died by the Lord's hand in Egypt! There we sat around pots of meat and ate all the food we wanted, but you have brought us out into this desert to starve this entire assembly to death."

They were seeking a quick way of escape instead of focusing on God's powers to overcome the situation. Instead of seeing that they were free, no longer slaves of Egypt, they are focused only on food. No doubt food is important, in fact, Abraham Maslow lists it as one of the basic needs but the Israelites missed the point. If God would bring them out of Egypt, He certainly would provide for all of their needs including food and water! Many of us are like the Israelites: when stress and problems come, we want the quickest, easiest path to escape even if that plan is far worse for us. Funny how that is not always God's plan.

Surely you think that an anointed king would trust God. But that is not what happened to Saul. He has been anointed by Samuel as king in 1 Samuel 10 and provided instructions to head to Gilgal and wait seven days. Then Samuel would come and they would sacrifice burnt offerings. But look what happens just a few chapters later:

> *1 Samuel 13:8-14 He (Saul) waited seven days, the time set by Samuel; but Samuel did not come to Gilgal, and Saul's men began to scatter. So he said, "Bring me the burnt offering and the fellowship offerings." And Saul offered up the burnt offering. Just as he finished making the offering, Samuel arrived, and Saul went out to greet him. "What have you done?" asked Samuel. Saul replied, "When I saw that the men were scattering, and that you did not come at the set time, and that the Philistines were assembling at Micmash, I thought, 'Now the Philistines will come down against me at Gilgal, and I have not sought the Lord's favor.' So I felt compelled to offer the burnt offering." "You acted foolishly, "Samuel said. "You have not kept the command the Lord your God gave you; if you had, he would have established your kingdom over Israel for all time. But now your kingdom will not endure; the Lord has sought out a man after his own heart and appointed him leader of his people, because you have not kept the Lord's command."*

Saul becomes impatient because God's timeline was not his timeline. Instead of waiting and following the command of God, Saul acted on his own. For Saul, he felt time was running out so <u>he</u> needed to act. We often do the same thing when we feel God is not moving fast enough. God often uses delays and barriers to test our obedience and patience with Him. For Saul, as us, the consequences of not trusting and following can be life changing impact.

In the very next chapter, we have a great example of what the outcome can be when you know and trust the promise of God. Ironically enough, we learn this lesson from Saul's own son, Jonathan.

1 Samuel 14:6-14 Jonathan said to his young armor-bearer, "Come, let's go over to the outpost of those uncircumcised fellows. Perhaps the lord will act in our behalf. Nothing can hinder the Lord from saving, whether by many or by few." "Do all that you have in mind," his armor-bearer said. "Go ahead; I am with you heart and soul." Jonathan said, "Come, then; we will cross over toward the men and let them see us. If they say to us, 'Wait there until we come to you,' we will stay where we are and not go up to them. But if they say, 'Come up to us, 'we will climb up, because that will be our sign that the Lord has given them into our hands." So both of them showed themselves to the Philistine outpost. "Look!" said the Philistines. "The Hebrews are crawling out of the holes they were hiding in." The men of the outpost shouted to Jonathan and his armor-bearer, "Come up to us and we'll teach you a lesson." So Jonathan said to armor-bearer, "Climb up after me; the Lord has given them into the hand of Israel." Jonathan climbed up, using his hands and feet, with his armor-bearer right behind him. The Philistines fell before Jonathan, and his armor-bearer followed and killed behind him. In that first attack Jonathan and his armor-bearer killed some twenty men in an area of about half an acre.

Jonathan and is armor-bearer know that God has promised them victory against the Philistines so they have no fear when they are outnumbered. Look at the trust and faith that Jonathan has when he says "nothing can hinder the Lord from saving, whether by many or by few." God's trust is able to overcome all fear even when you are outnumbered, or the debt is too big or the illness is too advanced. Regardless of the fear, your trust in God is always enough to overcome.

In Mark 10, we get a humbling look at what trust should be.

Mark 10:13-16 People were bringing little children to Jesus to have him touch them, but the disciples rebuked them. When Jesus saw this, he was indignant. He said to them, "Let the little children come to me, and do not hinder them, for the kingdom of God belongs to such as these. I tell you the truth, anyone who will not receive the kingdom of God like a little child will never enter it." And he took the children in his arms, put his hands on them and blessed them.

Jesus says; do not hinder the little children because they believe in Him without needing complete intellectual understanding. We do not need to understand everything in order to trust God. **Note**, a moment of self-reflection: this was one of the biggest barriers for me. In my journey of trusting and faith with God, my intellectual abilities was a huge hindrance. I knew God existed when I saw my children, an amazing sunset, the complexity of the human body but I wanted to see actual proof. I was constantly seeking something tangible but that's not what faith is based. It took me a long time to realize that trusting God is more about what I don't know than what I do know. If this has been a barrier for you may I suggest that you stop trying to be so analytical and trust in what you know: God loves you, He wants to spend eternity with you, you are not going to understand everything right now so stop trying to figure it all out and trust that he has a bigger plan for you.

Let's wrap up our look at trust by reviewing a passage from Romans.

Romans 3:21-31 But now a righteousness from God, apart from law, has been made known, to which the Law and the Prophets testify. This righteousness from God comes through faith in Jesus Christ to all who believe. There is no difference, for all have sinned and fall short of the glory of God, and are justified freely by his grace through the redemption that came by Christ Jesus. God presented him as a sacrifice of atonement, through faith in his blood. He did this to demonstrate his justice, because in his forbearance he had left the sins committed beforehand unpunished—he did it to demonstrate his justice at the present time, so as to be just and the one who justifies those who have faith in Jesus. Where, then, is boasting? It is excluded. On what principle? On that of observing the law? No, but on that of faith. For we maintain that a man is justified by faith apart from observing the law. Is God the God of Jews only? Is he not the God of Gentiles too? Yes, of Gentiles too, since there is only one God, who will justify the circumcised by faith and the uncircumcised through that same faith. Do we, then, nullify the law by this faith? Not at all! Rather, we uphold the law.

Paul just finishes giving all the bad news about how sinful we are and how we cannot earn salvation by upholding the law. He switches gears to share how we are saved from our sins: Trust in Jesus! All sin separates us from God. All the big one's we typically think like murder and adultery but the smaller one as well like hatred, lust, lying – they all separate us from God. However, this passage shows us that Jesus paid the price. Jesus <u>justified</u> us, declared us not guilty of our sins. We have <u>redemption</u> so that we can be free from the sin that binds us. We experience <u>propitiation</u> where the punishment of God has been removed from us. Because of our trust in Jesus we can move towards <u>sanctification</u> where we become more like Jesus through the Holy Spirit living in us. Trust in Jesus changes everything for us. The fear, hopelessness, anger, disappointment, despair and emptiness that we feel because of our separation from God is all restored through trust that Jesus paid the price and you have been restored.

Personal application

Throughout the interview, Steve and Ruth frequently came back to trust. Trust in God, His plan, His will for their life. These thoughts continue to expand on the complete trust they have in God.

- I think trust comes and grows as you know more about who God is and understand about His ways of doing things.
- As we read His word and understand how He called and used just ordinary people to accomplish His plan, we learn that we can trust Him to work in and through us.
- I think of the commitment we made to each other and God in our wedding. We trust Him to help us keep our commitment to each other and He has been faithful to see us through the past 44+ years.
- I also find I have to trust Him to protect our children and grandchildren, not just their physical bodies, but guarding their minds and hearts from the influence of the world.
- When I think about where this old world is heading, I have to trust Him to provide what is needed no matter what happens. The future can be overwhelming when I look at the attitudes of our culture.

- God has told us in His word that people are the same no matter what century they live in: there is selfishness, greed, hate, deception, violence and yet He has brought His people through those difficult days.
- He promises to give us what we need when we need it, and I pray that he will help me keep my eyes on Him and trust Him because He keeps His promises. He has done so over and over in the past and He is the same today and tomorrow so I can trust Him for the future.

CHARACTER AND IMAGE

Hebrews 11:39-40 All these people earned a good reputation because of their faith, yet none of them received all that God had promised. For God had something better in mind for us, so that they would not reach perfection without us.

What does character look like to you? What about image? If your response is that there is no difference, I hope to help you see how they are connected but different by the end of this chapter and certainly by completion of the book. Let's start with a working definition for each:

> Character: set of qualities you possess that make you distinctive, especially your qualities of mind, feeling and behaviors

> Image: the impression that others have of you, how you appear to others

Another way to think of character is who you really are on the inside. Your true thoughts and feelings; your beliefs and ideas; your desires and disgusts. Image is who you are on the outside. This is the part that you let others see, how they form an impression of who you are. This is where you only reveal certain characteristics to others because we all want people to like us and think favorably of us.

We can all think of a few examples. The TV evangelist who is preaching God's message and condemning sinners while involved in illegal dealings including drugs and adultery. The pro athlete who claims to never have used steroids but then test positive for the very

Character and Image

substance he never claimed to use. But it does not need to be someone in the public eye. Think of a co-worker, family member or better yet, look in the mirror. Our image, the one we show to others, is sometimes much different than what we truly know about ourselves.

What builds or influences character for you? Truly, it is a number of things. People in your life such as parents, siblings, teachers, friends, church leaders. But for some, it is people they never met including Hollywood stars, politicians, musicians and authors. Where you live, when you were born, money, where you go to school, race, sex, etc. all influence your character. Ironically all the things that influence your character also influence your image.

In Hebrews 11 we are provided a hall of fame of biblical individuals. These personalities demonstrated great faith and hope in God's word and promises. Yet each one hid their individual flaws and battle with sin and doubt. Abraham, Isaac, Jacob, Moses, David, Gideon, Samson and so many others endured pain and heartache; wanted to quit; struggled with sin and temptation yet even when they failed, they endured and overcame to continue their faith walk.

When we examine the lives of these biblical examples, we do not think they were perfect. We know they struggled with many of the same issues we struggle. We see to what extent they will go to protect their image—think David/Bathsheba. But we also know how God sees them: warriors of the faith. Their character was strengthened through every trial they endured. When they sinned, they sought forgivingness. When they were weak and hurting, they sought the Lord. Their character was developed from within and took a lifetime to build. As you see their character strengthen you see their image change. Your maturity in character has a profound impact on your outward image.

There are a few other clear examples worth mentioning as a point of reference. Go back and read the book of Ruth. Its only four chapters but in those few chapters we get an amazing look at the character of Ruth. Naomi, Ruth's mother-in-law, had lost everything. Her husband, two sons and now there is a famine in the land. She encouraged her two daughter-in-laws to return to their land and families but Ruth refused, stating that only death could separate her from Naomi. This is love in action, commitment, dedication, faithfulness and loyalty. Ruth's true character shown in her outward actions, her image.

Ruth 1:16-18 But Ruth replied, "Don't urge me to leave you or to turn back from you. Where you go I will go, and where you stay I will stay. Your people will be my people and your God my God. Where you die I will die, and there I will be buried. May the Lord deal with me, be it ever so severely, if anything but death separates you and me." When Naomi realized that Ruth was determined to go with her, she stopped urging her.

What about the character of Jonathan. There is not a great deal of time spent on Jonathan in the Bible but we learn amazing lessons about him in the little that is said. The deep friendship that he forms with David at the personal cost. Jonathan was next in line to be king following Saul but he knew that David had been anointed as the next king. Still, Jonathan loved David and longed for their friendship even while Saul was trying to kill David. We see David's character in response as he extends kindness to Jonathan's son, Mephibosheth, following Jonathan's death.

2 Samuel 9:1, 6-7 David asked, "is there anyone still left of the house of Saul to whom I can show kindness for Jonathan's sake?" When Mephibosheth son of Jonathan, the son of Saul, came to David, he bowed down to pay him honor. David said, "Mephibosheth!" "Your servant," he replied. "Don't be afraid," David said to him, "for I will surely show you kindness for the sake of your father Jonathan. I will restore to you all the land that belonged to your grandfather Saul, and you will always eat at my table."

There is no greater example of true character and matching image than God, who through Jesus, demonstrated His character traits of love, kindness and forgiveness in every single act, especially at the cross.

John 3:16-17 "For God so loved the world that he gave his one and only Son, that whoever believes in him shall not perish but have eternal life. For God did not send his Son into the world to condemn the world, but to save the world through him.

But let's spend a few minutes in detail looking at Paul and the change he experienced! Paul's character and image were extremely consistent. His character was made up of qualities that hated Christians. He had such a disdain for individuals that followed and accepted Jesus that he did everything possible to hunt, arrest, persecute and kill. There was no mistake; everyone knew exactly where Paul stood (his image). That is what made his transformation so powerful, but also so hard to believe.

Acts 9:1-22 Meanwhile, Saul was still breathing out murderous threats against the Lord's disciples. He went to the high priest and asked him for letters to the synagogues in Damascus, so that if he found any there who belonged to the Way, whether men or women, he might take them as prisoners to Jerusalem. As he neared Damascus on his journey, suddenly a light from heaven flashed around him. He fell to the ground and heard a voice say to him, "Saul, Saul, why do you persecute me?" "Who are you, Lord?" Saul asked. "I am Jesus, whom you are persecuting," he replied. "Now get up and go into the city, and you will be told what you must do." The men traveling with Saul stood there speechless; they heard the sound but did not see anyone. Saul got up from the ground, but when he opened his eyes he could see nothing. So they led him by the hand into Damascus. For three days he was blind, and did not eat or drink anything. In Damascus there was a disciple named Ananias. The Lord called to him in a vision, "Ananias!" "Yes, Lord," he answered. The Lord told him, "Go to the house of Judas on Straight Street and ask for a man from Tarsus named Saul, for he is praying. In a vision he has seen a man named Ananias come and place his hands on him to restore his sight." "Lord," Ananias answered, "I have heard many reports about this man and all the harm he has done to your saints in Jerusalem. And he has come here with authority from the chief priests to arrest all who call on your name." But the Lord said to Ananias, "Go! This man is my chosen instrument to carry my names before the Gentiles and their kings and before the people of Israel. I will show him how much he must suffer for my name." Then Ananias went to the house and entered it. Placing his hands on Saul, he said, "Brother Saul, the Lord—Jesus, who appeared to you on the road as you were coming here—has sent me so that you may see again and be filled with the Holy Spirit." Immediately, something like scales fell from Saul's eyes, and he could see again. He got up and was baptized, and after taking some food, he regained his strength. Saul spent several days with the disciples in Damascus. At once he began to preach in the synagogues that Jesus is the Son of God. All those who heard him were astonished and asked, "Isn't he the man who raised havoc in Jerusalem among those who call on this name? And hasn't he come here to take them as prisoners to the chief priests?" Yet Saul grew more and more powerful and baffled the Jews living in Damascus by proving that Jesus is the Christ.

Imagine you have known Paul for a long time. You did raids together, talked about hatred for Christians, and went to the lion matches on the weekends where Christians were slaughtered. Then the transformation occurs and he is not the same guy. Now he is one of the people that you have attacked previously and he is trying to win you over to Christ side.

Paul faced the challenge of needing to change his image. His character had been changed by God but now a lifetime of image was keeping him from showing his true character. But Paul knew to persevere. He was going to be beaten, tortured, imprisoned; jeered, flogged and chained yet he had hope that this world is not where his reward would be found. Like all the others mentioned in Hebrews 11, the reward was to be received later. They were all commended for their faith, their character, their image, regardless of how difficult the circumstances.

How do we go about changing our character and ultimately image if changes are needed? Romans 5 give us insight regarding how character can be changed:

Romans 5:1-5 Therefore, since we have been made right in God's sight by faith, we have peace with God because of what Jesus Christ our Lord has done for us. Because of our faith, Christ has brought us into this place of undeserved privilege where we now stand, and we confidently and joyfully look forward to sharing God's glory. We can rejoice, too, when we run into problems and trials, for we know that they help us develop endurance. And endurance develops strength of character, and character strengthens our confident hope of salvation. And this hope will not lead to disappointment.

For we know how dearly God loves us, because he has given us the Holy Spirit to fill our hearts with his love.

There is a process by which character can be changed. The character you are born with or currently have does not need to always be how you are defined. When you allow God into your life, changes occur. You now have access to Jesus through your faith and you start to understand how the hope in God affects you. You see God and His grace not only in the good times but especially during the trials and sufferings. You start to realize how God is changing, forming your character, showing you how to act, think and feel. We know that by overcoming the suffering we will persevere. By persevering through our crisis, we learn a bit more about ourselves thus impacting our character. This change in our character leads to hope and this hope now is what we show in our image.

When we go through a character evolution we change. The way we think about the world and other people. We start to look at relationships we have. As 1 Corinthians 15:33 states:

"Do not be misled: Bad company corrupts good character."

We desire to want to stop sinning and seek forgiveness for the countless sins we have committed. Our priorities start to change and yet we do not feel like we are losing anything, instead we are gaining everything.

Keep in mind this does not happen overnight and as your image starts to change you may get strange looks and questions from those that know you. Persevere, remain bold and consistent in how God is changing you! You will be persecuted and there will be challenges but you are a witness for the kingdom of God and your reward is not here. As Hebrews 11:25-26 reminds us: Moses chose to be mistreated along with the people of God rather than to enjoy the pleasures of sin for a short time. He regarded disgrace for the sake of Christ as of greater value than the treasures of Egypt, because he was looking ahead to his reward.

Personal Application

In a discussion regarding how one's character impacts the image they portray, Steve and Ruth shared the following:

- It is important that a Christian <u>live</u> their faith.
- As you grow and mature in your Christian faith, the character becomes part of your image; of which you are and not two separate things.
- There are times when demonstrating your faith publicly will be available. It is important to act on that opportunity and to build a public network of fellow Christians in your community and work.
- As others become aware of your Christian faith, it is important to always be aware that others are watching and hearing what you say and do and that might keep you from being able to be an effective witness.
- As they have experienced different groups where Christian faith is not present or evident, Steve and Ruth have been themselves, lived out their faith and found that they were integrated into the group without any repercussions. Living their faith did not keep them from having fun and participating with others. They discovered the key to this is to not expect others to live by your convictions – they aren't there yet. It's hard to be salt if you stay in the shaker or light if kept under a bushel.
- With maturity comes confidence to display your Christian character publicly and appropriately and therefore be genuine.
- As you are genuine and displaying your character publicly, you provide permission for others to show their true character through their image.
- It is important to look to others who you respect and who show their character through their image. These could be your parents, neighbors or older individuals in church but spending time with them is very valuable and allows time to soak in what they have to teach.

GODLY MEN

Matthew 12:35-37 A good man brings good things out of the good stored up in him, and an evil man brings evil things out of the evil stored up in him. But I tell you that everyone will have to give account on the day of judgment for every empty word they have spoken. For by your words you will be acquitted, and by your words you will be condemned."

It is well noted and documented in the decline of the family. In much of the research and in cases I have worked where there is an absent father or husband, the family is in trouble. The goal of this chapter is to show what God has to say about a man's role in society, church, marriage and raising children. I believe that if men followed the principles that God has outlined, the divorce rate would be lower, children would have a deeper relationship with God and lives you come in contact with would be changed.

For the past several decades the world view for people is to focus on self. For men this means a continued focus on how the world defines us. Therefore being successful in business, not just having a career but the pressure to be at the top of the rungs at any cost including sacrificing your marriage, children and faith. Look at the marketing that the world has designed to help us be successful: new improved golf clubs (which still has not helped my game); luxury sports cars for those who "have made it;" and don't forget that you are defined by your abilities when the "moment is just right." The world says live for yourself, life is short, do what you like and what makes you happy. Look at what Proverbs 14:12 states; seems pretty clear:

There is a way that seems right to a man, but in the end it leads to death.

But what if we, as men living in the world, lived according to God's instructions? In Matthew 12, Jesus teaches that a good man will bring out good things out of the good stored in him. Vice versa, a man who has evil in him will bring out evil things. Jesus goes on to say that one day each will give an account on the day of judgment. If the day of judgment is today would you be acquitted or condemned? These next few verses instruct as to how men should interact in the world:

Psalms 1:1 Blessed is the one who does not walk in step with the wicked or stand in the way that sinners take or sit in the company of mockers.

Proverbs 15:27 The greedy bring ruin to their households, but the one who hates bribes will live.

Matthew 5:14-16 You are the light of the world. A town built on a hill cannot be hidden. Neither do people light a lamp and put it under a bowl. Instead they put it on its stand, and it gives light to everyone in the house. In the same way, let your light shine before others, that they may see your good deeds and glorify your Father in heaven.

1 Timothy 2:1-6 I urge, then, first of all, that petitions, prayers, intercession and thanksgiving be made for all people—for kings and all those in authority, that we may live peaceful and quiet lives in all godliness and holiness. This is good, and pleases God our Savior, who wants all people to be saved and to come to a knowledge of the truth. For there is one God and one mediator between God and mankind, the man Christ Jesus, who gave himself as a ransom for all people. This has now been witnessed to at the proper time.

2 Timothy 2:1-3 You then, my son, be strong in the grace that is in Christ Jesus. And the things you have heard me say in the presence of many witnesses entrust to reliable people who will also be qualified to teach others. Join with me in suffering, like a good soldier of Christ Jesus.

1 Corinthians 9:22 To the weak I became weak, to win the weak. I have become all things to all people so that by all possible means I might save some.

We are to stay away from the wicked, refrain from being greedy, be an example to others, help others obtain the knowledge through Christ and become weak to save others. This seems contrary to what the worlds view is and thus an ongoing daily struggle to live in the world and yet maintain our commitment to God's word. However, we know that being strong and faithful to our teachings results in others learning about Jesus and strengthens our relationship with God.

In marriage, the Bible shares a great deal regarding our role as men. We have great responsibilities when it comes to our wife and the expectations are clear, so are the consequences. When a man marries, it is a natural progression that he will become one with his wife. They are to start a new family together as husband and wife. This means you leave your mother and father as Matthew 19:5-6 states:

'For this reason a man will leave his father and mother and be united to his wife, and the two will become one flesh'? So they are no longer two, but one flesh. Therefore what God has joined together, let no one separate."

Guys, if you are married but still clinging to your mother you need to stop. Your mom is not your wife and you will begin or continue to cause problems if you treat her as such. Your wife is to be honored, respected and loved. Colossians 3:19 reminds us:

Husbands, love your wives and do not be harsh with them.

Regarding sex, the world would have you believe that men are always ready to fulfill this responsibility. However, I have counseled many marital couples where the husband does not fulfill this role. Men, it is important that you do not lose interest or attraction to your wife. God's instruction on this is very clear:

1 Corinthians 7:2-5 But since sexual immorality is occurring, each man should have sexual relations with his own wife, and each woman with her own husband. The husband should fulfill his marital duty to his wife, and likewise the wife to her husband. The wife does not have authority over her own body but yields it to her husband. In the same way, the husband does not have authority over his own body but yields it to his wife. Do not deprive each other except perhaps by mutual consent and for a time, so that you may devote yourselves to prayer. Then come together again so that Satan will not tempt you because of your lack of self-control.

Take care of your body for it belongs to your wife. Do not deprive your wife for when sex does not occur you are inviting temptation to knock at the door of both you and your wife.

As men, we may have no greater impact in the world than as a father. Our society is faced with a huge epidemic in fatherless or absentee father homes. Let's define these a bit more: a fatherless home, for this purpose, is simple to define—there is no father present. This is the father that has left the home for any number of reasons but is gone has no parenting activities.

An absentee father is a bit harder to define. These dad's may be living in the home but "absent." You've seen these types before: they work extremely long hours to the point that they miss dinner almost every night. They miss ballgames and dance recitals. They are not there to help with homework or bedtime. Even on the weekends they are not "present" because they are working or involved in other activities. I have even seen dad's so involved at church that they become an "absent" father. When this happens your priorities are out of line and your family is going to suffer.

I'm not suggesting that you quit your job or stop serving at church. I am suggesting that you reexamine your priorities if you are an absent father. Answer a few of these questions honestly; ask your wife and kids if you are not sure of the answers:

1) Do you often miss family meals because of work?
2) Have you gone days at a time without seeing you kids because of work?
3) When you are home, are you actively engaged or need your own "down time?"
4) Have you missed ballgames, dance recitals, plays or school conferences because of work or other obligations?

5) Do you work even when on vacation?

6) Has your wife or kids said anything about why you are always gone?

If you answered yes to any of these questions then taking a quick look at your priorities may be in order. Keep in mind, this is not meant to be a guilt trip. As parents, we all go through periods where something comes up and we get tied up at work or there is another need. However, I'm talking about when your being "absent" is the norm, not the exception.

Let's look at some of the passages that the Bible mentions regarding fathers parenting their children and why it is so important that we are active, attentive and available for our children:

> *1 Timothy 5:8 Anyone who does not provide for their relatives, and especially for their own household, has denied the faith and is worse than an unbeliever.*
>
> *Proverbs 17:21 To have a fool for a child brings grief; there is no joy for the parent of a godless fool.*
>
> *Proverbs 23:24 The father of a righteous child has great joy; a man who fathers a wise son rejoices in him.*
>
> *Ephesians 6:4 Fathers, do not exasperate your children; instead, bring them up in the training and instruction of the Lord.*
>
> *Colossians 3:21 Fathers, do not embitter your children, or they will become discouraged.*
>
> *Hebrews 12:7-11 Endure hardship as discipline; God is treating you as his children. For what children are not disciplined by their father? If you are not disciplined—and everyone undergoes discipline—then you are not legitimate, not true sons and daughters at all. Moreover, we have all had human fathers who disciplined us and we respected them for it. How much*

more should we submit to the Father of spirits and live! They disciplined us for a little while as they thought best; but God disciplines us for our good, in order that we may share in his holiness. No discipline seems pleasant at the time, but painful. Later on, however, it produces a harvest of righteousness and peace for those who have been trained by it.

As father's we have a great responsibility to fulfill in bringing our children, the blessings God has given us, up in a home that knows and fears God; to understand what Jesus has done for us and the power of the Holy Spirit. The church and community can help your children know God but they will never have the influence you can as a model and teacher.

As we start to wrap up this chapter, I want us to look at a few verses regarding character that as men we should possess. In 1 Timothy, Paul is talking about the character of overseers and deacons but they should be the characteristics that all men hold:

1 Timothy 3:1-5, 8-9, 12-13 Here is a trustworthy saying: Whoever aspires to be an overseer desires a noble task. Now the overseer is to be above reproach, faithful to his wife, temperate, self-controlled, respectable, hospitable, able to teach, not given to drunkenness, not violent but gentle, not quarrelsome, not a lover of money. He must manage his own family well and see that his children obey him, and he must do so in a manner worthy of full respect. (If anyone does not know how to manage his own family, how can he take care of God's church?) In the same way, deacons are to be worthy of respect, sincere, not indulging in much wine, and not pursuing dishonest gain. They must keep hold of the deep truths of the faith with a clear conscience. A deacon must be faithful to his wife and must manage his children and his household well. Those who have served well gain an excellent standing and great assurance in their faith in Christ Jesus.

By following these guidelines, we will continue to mature and be the spiritual leader for our home that we have been instructed to do.

Let me close with Galatians 6:7-10 which is one of those passages that I wish I could remember in every situation:

Do not be deceived: God cannot be mocked. A man reaps what he sows. Whoever sows to please their flesh, from the flesh will reap destruction; whoever sows to please the Spirit, from the Spirit will reap eternal life. Let us not become weary in doing good, for at the proper time we will reap a harvest if we do not give up. Therefore, as we have opportunity, let us do good to all people, especially to those who belong to the family of believers.

We reap what we sow. You want to sow good and please God then stay strong, faithful and committed to God's word. If you want to live to please yourself and sinful nature, know that there are consequences for those actions and they will affect more than just you; they will impact your family, friends and community. Doing good does not always have immediate results. Do not think that life is a sprint; 500 mile race; best of 7 playoff series or final round at Augusta. If we don't give up, at just the right moment we will reap a harvest of good.

Personal Application

In this personal application, I wanted to know from Steve his thoughts regarding responsibilities being a Christian man. From Ruth, it is important to learn how being married to a Christian man has influenced her.

- It should be inherent for a man to want to provide for his family and live an upstanding life. Being a Godly Man builds the character and integrity of one's character; develops the morals and values to be more like Jesus.
- Becoming a Godly Man finishes what hopefully is started in one's youth. Is the continuation of the character that God starts in us at an early age.
- Ruth always knew where Steve's priorities were: God was first, family second and career followed. She did not need to worry that Steve was out doing something he shouldn't because he had the integrity of being Godly.

- Having priorities in order is very important and praying for wisdom and guidance can help ensure what the priorities are. (Hint: God is always first).
- Ruth would pray for Steve to be a good witness in the workplace. She would pray that he would show his true character and not sacrifice his beliefs for the career. She was rewarded for these prayers when Steve's manager commented positively regarding Steve demonstrating his Christian faith in the workplace.
- God will always honor have the right priorities.

RANDOM THOUGHTS

As the original thought for this book came from a study in Romans, I wanted to include some of the lessons learned that did not get a whole chapter but still very worthwhile to mention.

God's judgment is always fair.
Romans 2:11 For God does not show favoritism.

God's kindness leads us to repentance.
Romans 2:4 Or do you show contempt for the riches of his kindness, tolerance and patience, not realizing that God's kindness leads you toward repentance?

There are going to be several "but now" moments in your life. Since you have a relationship with God, have the Holy Spirit living in you and know the sacrifices that Jesus made for you, how are you going to respond to the "but now" moment listed in Romans 3:21-26?
Romans 3:21-26 But now a righteousness from God, apart from law, has been made known, to which the Law and Prophets testify. This righteousness from God comes through faith in Jesus Christ to all who believe. There is no difference, for all have sinned and fall short of the glory of God, and are justified freely by his grace through the redemption that came by Christ Jesus. God presented him as a sacrifice of atonement, through faith in his blood. He did this to demonstrate his justice, because in his forbearance he had left the sins committed beforehand unpunished – he did it to demonstrate his justice at the present time, so as to be just and the one who justifies those who have faith in Jesus.

Motivation is always easy to find when things are going well but what motivates you when there is trouble and pain? What will you hold on to as encouragement?

Romans 12:11-12 Never be lacking in zeal, but keep your spiritual fervor, serving the Lord. Be joyful in hope, patient in affliction, faithful in prayer.

Your body affects your behavior. Any change that you want to make requires energy and stamina to complete and maintain the change. Most of the changes we fail to make is because we do not have the energy do to so. Here are a few reminders regarding caring for your body:

Romans 12:1 Therefore, I urge you, brothers, in view of God's mercy, to offer your bodies as living sacrifices, holy and pleasing to God—this is your spiritual act of worship.

2 Corinthians 7:1 Since we have these promises, dear friends, let us purify ourselves from everything that contaminates body and spirit, perfecting holiness out of reverence for God.

Ephesians 5:29 After all, no one ever hated his own body, but he feeds and cares for it, just as Christ does the church.

1 Thessalonians 4:4 That each of you should learn to control his own body in a way that is holy and honorable

The law does not save you. When you hear others state that they will go to Heaven because they have been "mostly good" and not committed any big sins they are wrong! The law reveals our sins and brings consequences but it is Jesus who has saved us.

Romans 4:13 It was not through law that Abraham and his offspring received the promise that he would be heir of the world, but through the righteousness that comes by faith.

Do you limit God and put Him in a box? God, who created the universe and saved you from your sins, can do anything! Don't limit what He can do, dream big, expect God to exceed anything that you can possibly imagine.

Romans 5:10 For if, when we were God's enemies, we were reconciled to him through the death of his Son, how much more, having been reconciled, shall we be saved through his life!

We spent a whole chapter on sin but do not ever underestimate the power of the sinful nature. As Christians, we want to do good but we are always drawn to sin, it is a magnet. You have the desire to do good but not the power; Jesus is the answer.

Romans 7:21-25 So I find this law at work: When I want to do good, evil is right there with me. For in my inner being I delight in God's law; but I see another law at work in the members of my body, waging war against the law of my mind and making me a prisoner of the law of sin at work within my members. What a wretched man I am! Who will rescue me from this body of death? Thanks be to God —-through Jesus Christ our Lord! So then, I myself in my mind am a slave to God's law, but in the sinful nature a slave to the law of sin.

We all like to believe that we are in control of our life and actions but the truth is that there are very strong factors that influence us. Media, beliefs, politics and others have a great impact on the decisions we make and therefore the path we follow. When you have the Spirit of God in you, the mind begins to think differently.

Romans 8:5-8; 10-11 Those who live according to the sinful nature have their minds set on what that nature desires; but those who live in accordance with the Spirit have their minds set on what the Spirit desires. The mind of sinful man is death, but the mind controlled by the Spirit is life and peace; the sinful mind is hostile to God. It does not submit to God's law, nor can it do so. Those controlled by the sinful nature cannot please God. But if Christ is in you, your body is dead because of sin, yet your spirit is alive because of righteousness. And if the Spirit of him who raised Jesus from the dead will also give life to your mortal bodies through his Spirit, who lives in you.

Do you ever feel alone when going through a crisis? Even when you have friends and family around we can have a tendency to feel like no one is supporting us or willing to battle for us thus leaving us to struggle on our own. However, there is confidence in remembering that Jesus is always fighting for us.

Romans 8:34, 38-39 Christ Jesus, who died—-more than that, who was raised to life—-is at the right hand of God and is also interceding for us. For I am convinced that neither death nor life, neither angels nor demons, neither the present nor the future, nor any powers, neither height nor depth, nor anything else in all creation, will be able to separate us from the love of God that is in Christ Jesus our Lord.

As I continue down the path of spiritual maturity, I find myself completely in awe of God and what he has done. I realize that understanding everything the He does is not possible now but that is where faith and trust come to play. I do not always understand the path or His mind and definitely do not deserve the gifts. I am forever grateful for the wisdom and knowledge that He possesses for it makes His judgments fair even when I do not think they are.

Romans 11:33-36 Oh, the depth of the riches of the wisdom and knowledge of God! How unsearchable his judgments, and his paths beyond tracing out! "Who has known the mind of the Lord? Or who has been his counselor?" "Who has ever given to God, that God should repay him?" For from him and through him and to him are all things. To him be the glory forever! Amen.

Often we are faced with activities that are a matter of judgment. They are not listed as sins in the Bible but you know some Christians avoid (i.e. certain types of movies, music). There are eight tests that Tom Holliday mentions before participating in a particular activity:

1. Influence – will it hurt another believer
2. Prayer – have you spoke with Jesus about it
3. Reputation – will it hurt the reputation of the church or Jesus
4. Fellowship – will it hurt my relationship with a fellow believer
5. Appearance – does it look evil
6. Second coming – would you want to be doing the act when Jesus returns
7. Companion – would you want to do with another believer
8. Peace – is your heart at peace with the act

Romans 14:12 So then, each of us will give an account of himself to God.

An in-depth study of Romans is very worth the time and energy. There are so many lessons that Paul mentions and a good study guide will help connect all the dots.

BEGINNING

While this is the ending of the book hopefully it is a beginning or continuation of your spiritual walk with God. The topics we have discussed are things that we experience everyday sometimes multiple issues at one time. While temporary "relief" is found in different forms, if you want a complete healing your total trust and faith in Jesus is required.

The journey that you are embarking starting today will continue to be filled with pain, heartache, disappointment, fear and challenges. The reminders that you have read throughout these chapters should strengthen and encourage you and you in turn strengthen and encourage others. Have the confidence to know that your eternity is set so enjoy the ride of life and let your light shine when there is only darkness.

Do not think that just because you have read this book that you know all there is to know. It is vitally important for you to keep reading, studying and be involved in a bible teaching church and small group. You and I need to be fed daily and there is no acceptable excuse to not be involved in some sort of learning. I've tried all the excuses and when truth be told, if I don't spend some time with God each day it's because of my laziness or I think something is more important than God. I know schedules are busy and there may not always be time to study a lesson for 30 minutes but you can listen to Christian music in the car or iPhone; you can sign up for a daily devotional that comes to your inbox every morning that takes two minutes to read; you can always pray anywhere, anytime.

The God of the Universe, who created all things including you, loves you and desperately wants to have a close relationship with you. One of the greatest gifts He gave us is free will and I hope and pray that you use this gift to come closer to Him.

RECOMMENDED READINGS

The following is a list of books that has been compiled as good resources for the chapters in this book. I'm sure there are many more great resources that are not listed but this list would get you started on your journey and lead you to additional readings.

Character/Image
Into the Depths of God – Calvin Miller
The Owner's Manual for Christians – Charles Swindoll
The Good Life – Charles Colson

Doubt
The Benefit of Doubt: Encouragement for the Questioning Christian – Charles Swindoll
Getting through the tough stuff: It's always something – Charles Swindoll

Fighting Evil
Angels, Satan and Demons: Invisible Beings That Inhabit the Spiritual World – Robert Lightner
Disarming the Darkness – Calvin Miller

Giants
Facing Your Giants – Max Lucado

Grace
What's so Amazing about Grace? – Philip Yancey
Released from Shame: Moving Beyond the Pain of the Past – Sandra Wilson
The Grace Awakening – Charles Swindoll

Humility
Humility – Andrew Murray
Humility: True Greatness – C.J. Mahaney

Love
A Love That Never Fails – H. Dale Burke
I Promise – Gary Smalley

Parenting
Spiritual Parenting – Michelle Anthony
And Then God Gave Us Kids: How God Uses Our Kids to Help Us Grow – Tamara Boggs
The Light of Home: Ten Inspiring Pictures of a Strong Family – John Trent
Love-Powered Parenting – Tom and Chaundel Holladay
Bringing Up Boys – James Dobson
Bringing Up Girls – James Dobson

Patiently Waiting
Patience: The Benefits of Waiting – Stephen Eyre
Seven Spiritual Gifts of Waiting – Holly Whitcomb

Politics
Politics According to the Bible – Wayne Grudem
Red Letter Christians: A Citizen's Guide to Faith and Politics – Tony Campolo

Sin
Respectable Sins – Jerry Bridges
Jealousy: The sin no one talks about – R.T. Kendall

Trust
Created to Be God's Friend: How God Shapes Those He Loves – Henry Blackaby
Tokens of Trust: An Introduction to Christian Belief – Rowan Williams

Suffering
Holding on to Hope – Nancy Guthrie
Making Sense Out of Suffering – Peter Kreeft
Out of the Ashes: God's Presence in Job's Pain – Bill Crowder

Recommended readings

Our Ultimate Refuge: Job and the Problem of Suffering – Oswald Chambers

Story Telling

The Call: Finding and Fulfilling the Central Purpose of Your Life – Os Guinness

Tactics: A gameplan for discussing your Christian Convictions – Gregory Koukl

Godly Men

What Wives Wish Their Husbands Knew About Women – James Dobson

Coming Back to God: Answers to Men's Honest Questions and Doubts – Patrick Morley

Men's Secret Wars – Patrick Means

Additional Recommendations

Living the Psalms: Encouragement for the Daily Grind – Charles Swindoll

Sun Stand Still – Steven Furtick

Experiencing God: Knowing and Doing the Will of God – Henry Blackaby

The Faith – Charles Colson

CPSIA information can be obtained at www.ICGtesting.com
Printed in the USA
LVOW09s0004301113

363251LV00002B/8/P

9 781628 713510